I0014684

Blogging

Everything You Need to Know About Blogging From Beginner to Expert

(Proven Strategies to Launch Smart and Exponentially Grow Your Audience, Brand, and Income)

Matthew Cox

Published By **Region Loviusher**

Matthew Cox

Blogging: Everything You Need to Know About Blogging From Beginner to Expert (Proven Strategies to Launch Smart and Exponentially Grow Your Audience, Brand, and Income)

ISBN 978-1-998927-17-3

Legal & Disclaimer

Table Of Contents

Chapter 1: Finding your region of interest

You probably have a few pals with private blogs which can be smorgasbords of all their pursuits—images of their youngsters and film critiques and talk approximately their desired sports organization, and the whole lot in among. While that is outstanding for a personal weblog, in case you need to weblog professionally you have to slim your interest.

A blog that has a easy identity is much more likely to advantage success than one with a big popularity. A personal blog is prepared you at the same time as a professional weblog is set the topic. You can and must be personable and share your story, but nice because it relates to the difficulty at hand.

Before you begin doing something else to begin your weblog, you should discern out your difficulty rely. Your location of hobby will effect the domain name you pick out, the design of your net web web page, and your high-quality posting time table to attraction to the most readers on your place.

Research the market

Picking the right marketplace for a ultra-contemporary weblog may be complicated. You want to find out a topic that is well-known sufficient to attract hobby and earn cash, however one which hasn't already been oversaturated with bloggers giving their evaluations.

Finding a modern-day mindset on a subject, some issue that humans aren't already blogging about, gives you the high-quality threat of making it inside the industrial organization prolonged-term—if it's a subject in which interest exists, and the cause there aren't any bloggers on the topic isn't due to the truth no individual wants to have a look at approximately it. The only way to understand is thru learning the sphere.

The large the hobby in a given issue rely, the smaller percentage of the full market proportion you want to capture to obtain success, and the more specialized your location of hobby may be to offer a cutting-edge voice. Let's use a meals weblog as an instance. Food is a topic that hobbies a massive fashion of human beings—the general capability readership is large, however there are an consequently excessive massive kind of blogs already speakme approximately meals. Even in case you slim it down—say, to a weblog about cooking—you'll already discover masses of different blogs already doing that.

The interest in the location is so excessive you'll want to narrow it down again. Maybe you're a vegan and want to share recipes for making traditional consolation food that's vegan-friendly. You'll possibly find out there are pretty some vegan bloggers available, however the consolation meals mind-set will make you genuinely precise sufficient to be a new voice inside the communication, and there are sufficient human beings interested by the problem that every one of you can percentage the readership and be successful.

Now allow's say you have got were given a much less well-known problem matter—we'll use musical tool restore as an instance. Instrument repair is a sensible problem that lots of human beings is probably inquisitive about, from expert musicians to band administrators to people who play contraptions for fun, however it won't encompass pretty so massive a collection as cooking.

You would likely do the research and find out there are a number of musical device evaluation blogs, but no longer as many that focus on repair. Not simplest do you no longer need to interrupt your difficulty recollect down similarly into "wind tool restore" or "on the fly upkeep for rock musicians" however focusing on greater will probably slender your topic too much.

There isn't as a good buy opposition for device repair blogs as there may be for food blogs, however the group of involved readers is likewise smaller, this means that you need to attract a larger percent of interested readers to gain fulfillment.

Another manner to take into account this is to have a goal market period in mind numerically. Let's say you need to attain 1,000 unique subscribers. On the ground, the bigger intention marketplace seems to offer you the first-class statistical threat of being capable of find out extra readers. If there are one hundred,000 human beings interested by X and handiest 10,000 interested in Y, that would seem to offer you 10 times as many possibilities to make an effect on a totally unique reader.

But if 1,000 humans are already strolling a weblog about X and great ten are strolling a blog approximately Y this means that the smaller business enterprise will no matter the truth that have greater available readers consistent with blogger. With X, you'd ought to fight specific bloggers to dispose of a few percentage of their readership if you need to reach your goal; with Y, you can theoretically gain your purpose readership on the same time as not having to proportion readers with another blogger. The market can be smaller, however it's moreover an awful lot less saturated.

Of path, matters rarely exercising session that cleanly inside the actual international, however the very last aspect remains. The first-class place of interest for a today's blog in 2016 isn't always the only with the maximum essential following or the one that's the maximum particular; the nice vicinity of interest is the one that allows you to be a ultra-modern voice for a network for you to be able to assist you.

You shouldn't anticipate what shape of hobby exists on a given weblog situation rely earlier than you start doing all your research. Some subjects would possibly appear to be they'd be immensely well-known but turn out to be fantastically unusual while you've performed your studies, making them great capacity niches for you.

Conversely, you will possibly assume you're the simplest one inquisitive about a given concept, handiest to find the blogosphere already overrun with humans scribbling in your esoteric area of interest. Take notes as you do your studies to kill birds with one stone.

Bookmark blogs you need, both due to their appearance or the writing fashion of the author, then test the ones for mind as soon as your internet web web page is set up. If the blogs are in your niche, be part of up for their mailing listing, be privy to their posts, and recall commenting and grow to be a part of their network after you've were given your blog set up. It's by no means too early to start constructing goodwill (and properly conduct) to your running a weblog career.

Why you?

The weblog itself isn't always the product you're promoting to the purchaser. The blog web web page is extra much like the storefront. The merchandise which can be up on the market are your mind and expertise, as conveyed through your posts. To attraction to readers on your blog, you want to offer them a reason to concentrate to what you, specially, have to say about a given subject depend. Why would in all likelihood a person want to observe your weblog in preference to the ones already mounted?

For an instance, permit's use the challenge of professional baseball. There's a large target audience, but what rate do you need to offer to readers? Do you've got got an inner connection to the game enthusiasts? A new approach of assessment for the video games? Talking approximately how tons you need some element is probably a laugh for you, but it's now not very thrilling to look at.

The splendid bloggers have both a high degree of know-how approximately their subject matter or deliver a totally particular thoughts-set to the table. Even if a given region of hobby has a big potential target audience and not many competing voices, you won't attraction to any readers if you don't have some aspect interesting to mention approximately the situation. Before you are making your very last choice on which niche to delve into, ask yourself that easy question: why me? You need so that it will offer a one-sentence answer that would make someone interested by studying what you have got to mention.

Logistics

If your weblog suits certainly into your each day time desk and lifestyle, it'll be much less complicated that lets in you to located in the try of maintaining it, and you'll be a good deal much less probably to revel in crushed or give up due to burn-out. Make certain that the studies, writing, and advertising and marketing you'll want to do in your preferred location of hobby is sensible in your existence in advance than you agree on a subject. If you need to write down approximately the neighborhood tune scene, you'll should make a element of going to a number of shows—perhaps now not the outstanding concept when you have to evoke early each day for paintings.

If you want to put in writing a financial blog, you need as a manner to keep up with market tendencies and supply nicely timed recommendation on your readers who're relying on you to manual them via a brief converting panorama.

The area of hobby you pick out might also have an impact on the way you earn take benefit of your blog. If you're writing in a larger area of interest, your ratio of fly-with the useful resource of the use of web site traffic to copy readers is probably better. You'll get masses of web page perspectives that might appeal to advertisers, however can also additionally have a greater tough time selling products.

Conversely, a weblog in a small area of interest that has a loyal core of fanatics may not get as a bargain web website site visitors, however the in line with-traveler income may be better due to the fact the ones traffic buy products and services, whether or no longer they're precise to you or bought via an companion.

Blogging success tale: Joe Gilder

Joe Gilder is the proprietor of HomeStudioCorner.Com, a blog geared towards assisting people set up home recording studios. Within six months of beginning his blog, he had 500 subscribers on his electronic mail listing. By the time he sat down with Yaro Starak for his EJ Insider Interviews Club series, Gilder have become at the right music to make $three hundred,000 a three hundred and sixty five days, with thirteen unique profits streams all operating for him thru his weblog.

Gilder is an example of someone who's discovered fulfillment with the useful resource of focusing in on a pretty small area of interest. He doesn't have as many readers due to the fact the incredible-seemed "movie big name" blogs, however the readers he does have are greater dependable. More of his income is from his product range than it is from the conventional blog income sources, like advertising and associate programs.

He can preserve to make a residing through his blog despite the fact that he has a good deal less web site traffic than large internet sites due to the fact he makes more in step with traveler, supplying exquisite products that his readers advantage from attempting to find.

Chapter 2: Domains and website hosting

It can be tempting at the same time as you first start your blog to region it on a loose website online. After all, it's however a blog available at the internet, so why pay greater than you need to set up? Free weblog offerings are brilliant if you're a hobbyist, but they've vital dangers that may make your life a amazing deal tougher as a expert blogger.

Free web sites, in modern-day, don't rank as well in search engines like google as paid domains. They moreover don't offer you with as plenty manipulate over your design, making the internet web page look unoriginal and much less professional. Some loose offerings also run their personal commercials to your internet internet site on line, proscribing your chances of creating advert income.

Domain names

A area name is your address at the net (the part of the net website this is going between "www" and ".Com"). A new location call may be claimed through masses of specific on line services. A area that has been registered might not be off limits; a few people will purchase domain names to re-sell them no matter the fact that those are often a long manner greater steeply-priced alternatives.

It's not highly-priced to test in a modern-day vicinity call—doing it with GoDaddy can rate you as low as $10 a twelve months, and awesome services offer region registration inside the $20 to $40 range. Some domains are extra high-priced than others.

For a while even as the number one internet industrial corporation boom was taking vicinity, traders might also need to buy domains with the purpose of reselling them at a higher charge, with some going for masses or maybe tens of tens of millions of dollars (intercourse.Com supplied for $13 million in 2010, the modern file; making an investment.Com offered for $2.5 million in 2012). The bubble in this company has burst, however, or even the most in-name for domain names have visible their costs fall go into reverse to earth.

If possible, your location name want to in form the call of your blog. It doesn't ought to; at the same time as you very very very own your place call, you could placed a few component you need on that net internet site. Matching the internet address to the weblog call, even though, will give you greater call and brand recognition and make it less difficult for readers to discover you.

Think of some terms and phrases related to your location of interest and your mind-set on it. Once you've discovered a combination that you like, take a look at if it's to be had thru a web registration company. Generally talking, single-word titles (in particular those related to popular fields) are more likely to had been bought by means of the usage of using a domain investor and to charge extra cash to gather.

Let's use the example of the vegan comfort meals cooking blog from bankruptcy 1.

Cooking and vegan are not unusual phrases which is probably likely to be already used or, at the least, to were sold thru an investor. Think about the subsequent degree of your place of hobby, then—the comfort food mindset—and brainstorm possible mixtures.

Two and 3 word combinations are less in all likelihood to have been used already. With a hint creativity, you can discover an open location name that relates to your area of hobby and is greater quirky and remarkable than "VeganCooking.Com."

Hosting

Once your blog has a site call it has an deal with, but it doesn't however have a domestic. The files associated with your internet internet site on line will want to be hosted on a server in order that your site visitors can get right of entry to them. There are many web hosting web sites available. Many locations that check in domain names furthermore offer net hosting offerings, that is reachable, although you need to ensure the internet

internet web page has the offerings you want earlier than signing up. Blue Host is a commonplace net website hosting net net web page for WordPress bloggers who're transitioning to a self-sufficient web website on line.

The maximum important trouble to keep in mind is how a remarkable deal net web website online visitors quantity you may have on a particular hosting website. Bandwidth limits received't consider while you're first beginning your blog, however if you wish to enlarge your traffic quick, you shouldn't set yourself up for failure thru selecting a server that's too small. A lot of internet net hosting sites offer unique ranges of packages at wonderful fees relying on your internet web page traffic desires and make it easy to beautify down the road.

You can usually pay for website hosting month by means of the use of month and at the same time as you usually get a piece of a discount for buying greater time right now, paying month-to-month can will let you strive a company out in case you're now not excellent whether or now not it's far going to provide you the results you want. Moving hosts may be a problem however isn't as high priced or difficult as changing domains is probably; you could change your mind inside the destiny with out affecting your reader's ability to access your pages.

When you're first beginning out, the cheapest choice is mostly a shared net hosting account. Prices can begin as low as $1-$2 in line with month. Sites that offer this option encompass iPage, eHost, and In Motion Hosting. Research the web hosting internet site on line in advance than you sign on. Are they reliable, or do you see users complaining about their provider? You also can test spherical with super bloggers and be conscious what net website hosting web sites they use. Site builders and CMS

You've were given a website call and a bunch wherein the documents related to it is able to stay. Now all you want to do is make your blog and transfer it to the host—and if you're no longer a technically-minded individual, this could be very intimidating.

The diploma of involvement you need to have with the creation of the internet web page code for your net web site will determine which kind of internet site online editor or internet site builder is first-class for you. People use the ones phrases in notable methods, inclusive of to the confusion.

A net editor offers you the most control over your net web page's format, but furthermore requires some expertise of HTML and CSS, and probably furthermore things like JavaScript, PHP, and Perl for the form of additives most human beings want on a weblog. The most easy net editor is a undeniable text software like Notepad. Plain textual content applications will require you to write down down down all of the code, however are the cheapest and most straightforward choice.

Web editor applications like Dreamweaver and KompoZer have a visible interface for the purchaser, making the internet net page building experience more much like designing a Word document than to writing computer code.

Once you've designed your pages with a web editor, you still need to get them onto your host's server the use of an FTP (File Transfer Protocol) software program application. Both the FTP software application and the net editor will want to be established on your laptop, and you've got complete control over their use—the number one benefit of the use of this technique.

An online internet site online builder is just like a internet site editor besides run absolutely online in vicinity of via your computer. Site builder offerings are provided with the resource of huge net internet web website hosting businesses (which encompass GoDaddy) despite the fact that often for a in addition rate. The on line internet site on line clothier might also have a similar interface as a web editor like Dreamweaver or KompoZer. Since you're constructing your sites right now at the host, despite the fact that, you don't have to worry about uploading them with an FTP software program, and you could use any tool to edit your internet site, now not most effective one pc with the software hooked up.

Even in case you're the use of internet website enhancing software or an internet net internet site online builder, primary knowledge of as a minimum HTML and CSS can be very beneficial in making your net web page look and feel the manner you want. Even if you don't apprehend the way to code them, you need to understand what they do and be capable of interpret them even as you see them.

A Content Management System (CMS) is a chunk of software program software software program you install proper away for your internet host (now not your laptop) that streamlines the addition of important website talents like tags and classes for pages, search and archive talents, or forums and remark sections.

When you use internet web web page developers or net website online editors, every of those features will should be introduced manually, which can be alternatively time-ingesting even if you are a web coding expert. Content control structures additionally make it masses less complicated to convert the advent of your not unusual net web web page.

CMS software program software does absorb region to your server and web websites run with a CMS use more RAM and CPU than the ones made by way of the usage of a domain editor. On excessive traffic days, this may suggest your pages are gradual to load or can also want to cause problems with aid limits if you're the usage of a shared server.

You additionally don't get pretty as an awful lot revolutionary manage over the competencies and format factors of the net page as you may designing it truly to your very very own. The essential advantage of CMS software program program is that it lets you attention at the content material. You don't have to worry approximately solving strains of code or manually adjusting your pages whilst you make a decision on a extremely-current format—that means you've got were given extra time to art work on the vital subjects.

There are severa blogger-particular CMS applications at the internet, a whole lot of which you may use with out fee. WordPress is probably the most common. I understand what you're thinking—isn't WordPress this sort of loose walking a weblog net sites? It can be (WordPress offers free weblog web hosting), however you could moreover down load it as software program program software program and set up it to your area.

It's in reality now not the satisfactory product to be had available on the market, no matter the fact that; take it gradual and punctiliously bear in mind what abilities you'll ideally need. Just like with changing domain names, changing CMS software application program can be a headache and a half of when you have to do it down the street.

If you take component in the ebook so far, please allow me understand.

Blogger achievement tale: Ruhul Amin

Ruhul Amin is the founder of Tips and Tricks HQ, an Australian-based totally weblog geared closer to instructing specific bloggers approximately WordPress and other technical factors of jogging a weblog. Not exceptional is his web website on-line impeccably designed and honestly a success, however it could moreover be a precious resource for trendy bloggers who aren't so wonderful on the technical side of things.

Amin stresses the importance of a best region name in his posts, and has some recommendations for readers: use key phrases, make it clean to preserve in mind, and preserve it short. Amin advises, "It is critical for a traveller to get an idea of what the internet net web page is prepared simply thru looking on the area name…if [visitors] can't keep in mind the region name then you run the threat of losing potential visitors."

One more tip from Amin: consider that you may use hyphens amongst terms in domains if it allows with the overall readability as he does on his internet site (www.Tipsandtricks-hq.Com). Not most effective can this make the decision of your blog clearer to net website online visitors, however it could also be a way to get the appropriate domain name if the un-hyphenated version was offered.

Chapter 3: Building your brand

Your logo is the muse of your weblog's identity and cause. In his article "7 suggestions of a fulfillment bloggers," Robert Pagliarini defines your brand as "the emotional response a person feels while she or he concentrate your name." You have a emblem right now, even in case you don't understand it—in truth, you in all likelihood have numerous.

You have a positive logo even as you're at artwork, some other at the aspect of your circle of relatives, possibly even awesome ones with severa organizations of buddies. For many new bloggers, that's a part of the trouble. Your actual-existence manufacturers are too diverse and scattered to make for a compelling weblog; you want to narrow and craft your emblem into a salable bundle deal deal.

A logo is a aggregate of your character and your reputation. Your personality is the way you try and present yourself to others; your recognition is fashioned via the way you've got interaction with them. When you're first starting out as a weblog and haven't however built a reputation, you're going to be running off of the electricity of your man or woman on my own. It's important, then, to decide what your emblem can be earlier than you begin writing your posts, and then to beautify that brand always via your content.

Play to your target market

Imagine your perfect reader. Think about how they spend their time. Are they unmarried, or do they have got a circle of relatives? Where do they stay? What are their values? Tailoring your emblem to your goal market can assist provide you with a higher recognition in your first few posts and permit you to installation your identification greater fast.

Of route, you shouldn't take this too a long way, each. Don't fake to be a modern-day individual virtually to attract greater readers. You're no longer converting your man or woman, absolutely figuring out which elements of it'll in all likelihood be the maximum attractive to your purpose reader. Consider it this manner: even as you're at artwork, you in all likelihood get dressed in a selected manner, have a terrific bearing, and use a first rate vocabulary than even as you're setting out together with your buddies on the bar or looking TV with the kids at home.

All the ones versions of yourself are "you," you're in reality tailoring them to the state of affairs. Most humans do this subconsciously in reaction to the non-verbal cues and clues in their environment. With running a blog, you could't see the people you're interacting with; without those context clues, it's vital to construct the character you want to apply in place of letting your unconscious do it for you.

Think approximately your super photograph. Do you need to be a pleasing confidant? A informed expert? Think decrease lower back to the "why me?" query you spoke back in financial wreck 1. If the motive you selected your place of interest is because of the reality you've studied that subject matter and characteristic severa records to share, your logo might be geared in the direction of teaching your readers.

That branding gained't paintings if you're a relative beginner in your topic region; perhaps alternatively your logo can be reading the way to come to be a better chef, or finding the splendid attractions for your town, and bringing the reader alongside in your discoveries.

If you're having trouble considering what you need your logo to be, a few old fashioned brainstorming can also really do the trick. Get out a smooth piece of paper and a pen. Write "I want my weblog to be…" massive on the pinnacle of the paper, then write down some component phrases come to thoughts. Link those terms collectively into thoughts and sentences, rearranging and connecting them until you revel in together with you've gotten to the coronary heart of what you're looking for to represent.

You've in all likelihood heard the time period "elevator pitch," a description of your product or concept that might be conveyed in the time it takes to adventure in an elevator— about thirty seconds, in case you want to place pretty a number on it. Before you begin strolling a blog, you ought at the way to offer an elevator pitch of your emblem and problem count. Once you can do this, you ought to have a easy sufficient idea of your logo to stay regular via your early posts.

The importance of format

The layout and format of your weblog will supply your reader their first affect of you. On the sensible component of factors, you need to make sure it's each smooth to navigate and smooth to observe. Important posts need to have a excellent area on the net internet web page, and the coloration scheme shouldn't intrude with the legibility of your writing.

A pre-made template like the ones to be had on WordPress may be an exquisite region to begin whilst you're designing your weblog, but you should customise at the least some factors of it to help it stand happy with the lots of others that use that same format. The format you pick out on your blog need to in some manner reflect your emblem or place of interest. Ideally, a reader need if you want to glance at your internet page without studying a word and get a easy concept of your weblog difficulty remember quantity.

Layout and colour alternatives have a few feature on this; if you run a images weblog, you need to choose out a format that emphasizes pix, as an instance. Consider specialized features. A monetary weblog may additionally locate it useful to install a live tracker of the inventory alternate on their the the front web web page; a sports activities activities blogger would possibly have a ticker of rankings and in form effects.

A excellent way to make clear your brand is to format a emblem that shows every your vicinity of interest and your individual. You can do this your self in case you're creative, however for plenty human beings, it's worth the monetary investment to hire a freelancer to format the logo for you. The brand will come to symbolize your logo in maximum readers' minds, and the initial funding you're making hiring a designer may be repaid commonly over thru way of the growth for your brand reputation.

Though this is maximum vital together at the side of your logo, it is able to moreover be actual of numerous components of your weblog design. If you want custom designed pics or a very specific format layout but don't have the design or coding historical past to cause them to nicely your self, don't be afraid to search for a freelancer to complete the be virtually proper for you. A properly-designed internet site on line may be more likely to attract site visitors and will in the long run be absolutely worth the initial financial funding.

Blogging success story: Nicola Lees

Nicola Lees had already built a a achievement profession in tv earlier than she commenced TVMole.Com. She developed a strong logo based totally totally on her statistics, supporting human beings with mind for TV suggests to pitch those suggests to TV executives and manufacturers.

The content on TVMole all reinforces this robust logo, giving beneficial advice that readers can't get everywhere else, permitting her weblog to boom and expand into a couple of profits streams. She does are trying to find recommendation from and agreement work, speaks on panels and sells books and guides that assist her readers.

Having labored with crucial organization leaders similar to the BBC and Discovery Chanel intended Lees' apparent preference come to be to base her logo spherical her know-how. Her insider attitude makes her a trusted voice in the location of interest of television production.

But no matter the reality that she had the credentials, it emerge as although Lees' notable and honest content material material that bolstered her brand on her blog and helped her generate web site traffic and opportunities.

Chapter 4: Planning and Goals

When a person's getting ready to begin a brick-and-mortar small enterprise organisation, she or he are frequently suggested to offer you with a business plan earlier than she or he even find out funding or search for a vicinity. Because of the portions of cash involved, customers need to recognise that the owner has perception approximately each thing of their commercial employer— and most importantly, has planned out how it'll make coins and grow—earlier than they are willing to back the concept.

While you don't want to hustle for customers whilst you're starting a blog, a bit of purpose-orientated making plans continues to be the first-class manner to make your blog a worthwhile task as opposed to simplest a hobby and time-sink.

Remember that during a single day successes are very uncommon, now not actually in running a blog however in each location of life. The artwork you put in at the begin of the gadget may not start to generate returns till a 365 days or greater has exceeded. If you're no longer geared up to play the lengthy game, you're possibly to surrender too quickly and by no means see your blog reach its whole potential.

You gained't need to make investments a bargain coins in beginning a blog, however you may want to devote some time constantly sufficient to be visible as dependable by means of way of way of your readers. Schedule yourself at least an hour to work on your weblog each day. Commit to it as lots as you may shift at your place of employment. If you don't cope with your blog discover it impossible to resist's important, you may't anticipate the readers to revel in any in each other manner.

Setting practical goals

Everybody would love to be growing a six-determine income from domestic talking approximately taken into consideration one in all your passions. That's not an unrealistic goal in the prolonged-term. The problem is that plenty of human beings anticipate they'll start a blog and inner some months make sufficient to retire. When they don't accumulate this top of success right away, they get discouraged and give up.

Setting practical goals doesn't advocate you can't dream huge. It instead manner breaking the ones large dreams down into pieces and identifying what quick-term steps you can take to gather lengthy-term achievement.

First of all, you have to decide really what your long time dreams are. Where does jogging a weblog in shape into your perfect destiny? Is it some element you in the end wish to apply as your number one deliver of income or do you be aware it as clearly one part of a bigger complete? The quantity of attempt you'll ought to mounted to assemble a weblog right into a whole-time task can be very precise than what is going to be required just to make some spending cash on the aspect.

If you very very very own a small employer or product line, a weblog may be extra your way of speaking at the facet of your clients than it is your primary deliver of earnings—an crucial a part of the whole package, but not your essential earnings flow into. If you do want to make jogging a weblog your full-time hobby, you want to address it like a element-time hobby from the outset; if it's supposed as a aspect challenge, you can take greater time to allow it expand.

Once you've notion about your long-time period dreams, do some studies on one-of-a-kind blogs on your area of interest. Start with the useful resource of looking on the maximum a fulfillment and maximum famous ones. How many web page perspectives and feedback do maximum of them get?

How frequently do they positioned up? How many enthusiasts do they have got on Facebook and Twitter—and the manner extended has it taken them to get up to now? If the top weblog on your area of interest has

3,000 enthusiasts, placing a reason of five,000 followers on your first six months might maximum probable quality set your self as an entire lot as fail. Set smaller milestones. If you want 1,000 subscribers, you first need to get 100 subscribers. Then you may cross for 500, and so on, presenting you with benchmarks of success to hit along the manner.

Scheduling your posts

There are two tiers to keep in thoughts proper right here, and also you want to chill animated film out a plan for each before you begin writing your content material. There's the week-through-week scheduling of even as you want your posts to come out, and there's the monthly and yearly scheduling of factors or activities you want to hit.

A lot of bloggers absolutely located up at the same time as the spirit moves them. They would possibly have 4 posts in three days after which a -week hole till the subsequent one. That's fine if you're a hobbyist or if the weblog isn't your primary profits flow, however to make your weblog profitable, it's higher to keep a ordinary time table on which your readers can rely. Exactly whilst you post will depend on your location of interest.

News-based totally blogs may additionally moreover additionally need to be up to date every day to enjoy modern-day-day. For much less time-sensitive topics, you may select select days of the week. As always, don't forget your target market. A business blog might probable want to have a put up of their subscriber's inboxes each weekday morning; e-mails sent over the weekend can be lots much less in all likelihood to be regarded.

A blog approximately nightlife inside the town might want to place out a big positioned up on Thursday on the equal time as subscribers are making plans for the weekend. Whatever your area of interest, a weekly time table we must your readers recognise once they need to expect to pay interest from you and will more correctly gather a strong subscriber base.

The every year scheduling may be extra beneficial for coping with your content material cloth and identifying the times interest to your niche may be maximum. Some of those gadgets can be popular—any blogger who sells merchandise should make be aware of the Christmas purchasing season on their every yr calendar—but many might be greater person to your vicinity of hobby.

A gardening blog ought to possibly want to time a ultra-modern product release to correspond with overdue wintry climate or early spring at the same time as masses of readers might be planning their gardens. A parenting blog might also want to have special content fabric for decrease lower back to high school season. By writing it all out, you may greater absolutely see what factors in the 12 months you want to assemble inside the path of and in which you could have a more difficult time developing with content material fabric, allowing you to plot because of this.

Collaboration

Collaboration with every different blogger may be an easy way to maintain the net web page taking walks easily at the same time as at the identical time spreading out the pressure and the workload concerned in keeping it. It we need to each of you take time off while you need to, and can also help to feature greater perspectives to the blog's content material material fabric, growing its attraction. Just make sure you choose your taking factor companions cautiously.

It ought to be someone you get along issue, but moreover a person you can assume to do their sincere percentage of the art work. Ultimately, the motive is for this to be a profitable enterprise enterprise mission, and you need to make certain from the outset that everybody worried is on the identical page and committed to that motive. Even if the person is a family member or near buddy, it's a outstanding idea to install writing down up and signal an settlement together simply to make sure the expectations are smooth.

Blogging success tale: Lance Nelson

When Lance Nelson determined to begin his blog, he picked a very specific region of interest. Banskoblog.Com is within the Bansko ski hotel in Bulgaria. Nelson grew to grow to be this pretty constrained place of hobby right right right into a complete-time mission that brings in over 60,000 euros in line with one year in earnings, and his successful branding had masses to do with the rate and diploma of his achievement.

Everything on his internet site on line, from the mountains on his emblem to the weather tracker widget and menu alternatives, clearly tells the reader honestly what he is set, and this precise branding paid off for him in a big manner.

Being a skiing blogger way that Nelson has to assume very cautiously about the scheduling of his content. His readers are going to be most interested by the direction of the skiing season, and he has a organized-made aim market inside the iciness; his venture changed into a manner to keep his readership in the summer season months when there's no snow for snowboarding.

Nelson posts approximately different subjects inside the summer time which might be of interest to his readers. He travels inside the path of Bulgaria and stocks his travels together together with his readers (who can also themselves be searching out a few element to do at some stage in the summer season, because they're able to't ski). Even if you're not in this form of weather-hooked up area of interest, considering what your best readers may be doing in some unspecified time in the future of the 12 months will will let you discern out the right content material cloth for the immediate.

The Art of Blogging

There are three essential elements in a blog's achievement: The super of the content material fabric cloth, the dimensions of the target marketplace, and the way well it's networked into the community. The the kind of that you as a blogger have the maximum manage over is the content material material material itself. Though there are subjects, you could do to boom the scale of your readership and make networking contacts if your content isn't as loads as snuff you received't be able to assemble a devoted target market or get one manner links from one among a type blogs regardless of how aggressively you put it on the market your product.

Remember usually to consider your target audience and take note of the tendencies taking place to your niche on every occasion you're operating on your weblog, whether that's writing a put up or interacting together with your readers. Something that works for a political weblog may not be as well-best for a gardening weblog, and vice versa. Variety is likewise critical to maintaining your reader's hobby.

If you can, transfer up the lengths of posts and the ratio of snap shots to textual content now and then. A style blogger may additionally comply with up an prolonged piece on a modern-day show she attended with a short blurb about a ultra-modern purse from her desired designer. Be as present day and open-minded with the fashion of your posts as you are with the content material cloth.

Chapter 5: Quality content

You've probably heard in advance than that "content material cloth material is king," and it's real. Quality content material cloth fabric is what is going to assemble your following and convey opportunities for profits and enlargement. You want the posts for your weblog to offer rate for your reader and to be thrilling to test. It should additionally be professional and free of distracting mistakes. Readers will normally forgive the errant typo or verb disagreement, but it'll be more difficult to steer your reader to accept as actual with you in case you normally have problems with English mechanics.

The spelling and grammar checker on your phrase processor will capture most mistakes; even if you're confident to your writing ability, run it on each post earlier than it's miles going as a good deal as put off silly typos and mistakes. If you recognize, spelling and grammar are hard for you, get a replica of The Elements of Style via way of William Strunk and E.B. White. Give it a look at then maintains it on the desk in that you'll be going for walks, to are looking for advice from at the equal time as needed.

The best length of a modern-day blog put up is spherical 3 hundred-seven-hundred phrases. It ought to have a headline that makes the reader need to click on on on it (despite the fact that be wary of "click on bait" style titles which might be deliberately misleading). The content material ought to have a logical go along with the go with the flow, with main thoughts in reality highlighted in bulleted lists or separated paragraphs.

When you first begin your weblog, all of the posts you located up need to be at once related to your location of interest. You want to carry your brand from the begin, so readers understand what to anticipate from you. You additionally want to demonstrate your data approximately the sector you're writing in— to set up your know-how with the priority, and display readers why they must care approximately your evaluations.

Your first 10-15 posts should be without delay related to your area of interest. Some very a hit bloggers do every now and then burst off-situation matter, but that have to wait till you've mounted your identity.

Core content fabric fabric

Blogging professional Yaro Starak talks about a few component referred to as a "pillar article" in his advice columns. Chris Garret calls it "flagship content material," while Brian Clark calls it "cornerstone content fabric fabric." All of these specialists are describing the equal number one detail: the articles that deliver your reader a smooth idea of your location of interest and your opinions about it.

Core content material articles ought to be on the lengthy thing—spherical 500-1,000 terms, relying on the layout. These posts need to not be time primarily based totally; a reader who sees the positioned up a 3 hundred and sixty five days from now must however discover it to be relevant. These posts are the maximum probable to gain inbound links from different websites and preferably will maintain to usher in new readers extended whilst you to begin with placed up them.

So they don't get buried to your records, it's a first rate concept to list these posts in a separate region, whether or not that's a drop-down menu or hyperlinks in a sidebar—this we could new readers effortlessly get proper of access to the most beneficial content material fabric cloth. You also can reference these articles your self in destiny posts to help new readers discover and look at them.

The extra of those center content fabric posts you embody on your weblog, the higher. Five is a brilliant minimal, and also you want to encompass as a minimum for your first ten posts. The ultimate goal of any well center content material fabric submit is to educate your readers a few element, whether or not or now not it's a understanding associated with your niche, a proof of a idea, or an opinion piece as a way to assist them see your area of interest in a brand new way. If you're now not positive what form of article to write, a few middle content material cloth options are indexed under, and can assist provide you with an idea of wherein to start.

Glossary pages are lists of terms associated with your vicinity of hobby which you define for the reader for your non-public phrases. Glossary pages are often a beneficial tool if your region of hobby is related to technology, finance, regulation, or any other discipline that has very specific or esoteric terminology. They're additionally a wonderful layout for purchasing once more-links due to the reality exclusive blogs would in all likelihood reference your net web page inside the event that they don't have word listing pages in their non-public.

Step-thru-step how-to articles educate your reader the manner to do a challenge or make a product, frequently with pictures at key steps. Recipe posts on cooking blogs wholesome into this beauty and are likely the most familiar example, however this article fashion applies to nearly any place of interest. Think of something in your business enterprise which you realize a way to do and your readers may not—the critical element element proper proper right here is sharing your information of some thing with that you're skilled.

Whitepapers are much like how-to articles however bypass into greater intensity. A whitepaper is generally a 2-10 web page document that teaches readers approximately a concept or subject matter related to your industry. It ought to be an all-encompassing approach to a common hassle on your niche. Rather than being a single prolonged weblog placed up, it's frequently pleasant to provide whitepapers as PDFs readers can down load. You may additionally moreover kind the content fabric into numerous blog posts and hyperlink them collectively in a sequence. List articles are brilliant middle content cloth because of the truth people love to have a look at and percentage them, and they may be top for stirring up a conversation on your announcement segment. They can take some office work. Advice lists supply readers tips on the way to carry out obligations ("four processes to get higher sleep" or "5 activities earlier than you get a mortgage"). Ranked lists are perfect for popular subculture or product-based blogs, which can also hyperlink to merchandise offered by the usage of using an affiliate to increase the component's profitability. Informative lists percentage know-how with the reader ("most underneath-rated horror movies" or "wonder advantages of inexperienced tea") and can be beneficial in any place of hobby.

Opinion portions and editorials are most customarily seen in political and social statement blogs, and may be in particular beneficial for stirring up controversy to your feedback phase. These portions must begin with a clear thesis statement, whether or not or not that's a principle, an opinion, or an hassle. Back up your argument with properly-offered arguments and ensure the idea is particular—bear in mind, you want to characteristic new price for your organisation, not rehash the same thoughts offered some region else. Also, ensure your opinion reinforces your set up logo.

search engine advertising

seek engine advertising stands for Search Engine Optimization, and the way important it is to getting right consequences in search engines like google like google and yahoo like google and yahoo remains up for debate within the jogging a blog network. The idea of seo is that with the useful useful resource of using key phrases in the direction of your posts, you could get better ratings on consequences lists on the equal time as customers search for those phrases, which means you'll get more visitors on your internet internet web page. Nobody debates that this is a few issue to help you; what blogging professionals disagree on is how masses you need to recognition honestly to your key-word density.

If you're writing correct content material material that's strongly related to your niche problem matter range, your posts will glaringly be very key-phrase-dense without you putting in any particular attempt. An over-emphasis on key-phrase density may want to make your posts feel repetitive or stilted. Putting way too many key phrases for your posts additionally makes you appear like a spammer (called "key-word stuffing") and makes are looking for engine spiders forget about approximately about you in case you're accountable of it.

The maximum critical places to emphasize key phrases for your posts are in the internet net page header and the perceive tag. When you're naming your pages, lead them to go looking engine in a pleasing manner by way of the use of giving them names that simply explicit what the net internet page is ready in choice to an in-residence class tool. Keep the content fabric cloth itself centered on the concept and don't worry masses about getting terms shoved in there—if it's on the topic in your vicinity of interest, it'll stand up in trying to find outcomes truely. A better manner to optimize your are seeking engine rating is to link lower decrease returned to your personal pages periodically.

The extra links a web internet web page has to it, the more likely it is to reveal up higher at the search end result list. Just like with the important thing phrases, don't over-do it. Reference past posts while it's logical to accomplish that, now not most effective for the sake of search engine advertising.

Finding your voice

Many people make the mistake of trying to offer a really perfect photograph of themselves to their readers. While you do want to offer your self as someone the reader can trust, you furthermore mght want to expose them that you're a actual individual. There are lots of blogs out there approximately each state of affairs depend attainable, and in the long run your persona and reviews are what's going to make your weblog the only readers need to study.

Be inclined to proportion your disasters, disturbing situations, and struggles. It will make you greater relatable, and the reader will in the end endure in mind you greater within the occasion that they realize you're the sort of individual who can admit in your mistakes.

A correct blog positioned up should have the tone of a communication among friends. If you're now not certain absolutely the manner to do that, there are more than one tips you may attempt. Try imagining that you're speakme to a person in your lifestyles, like a sibling or a chum, when you write your posts. How would probable you supply an explanation for standards for your area virtually so your sister can recognize them? Use the identical language while you're writing which you'd use out loud in quality conversation.

Especially in case you're not a trained creator, phrases like "voice" and "tone" can on occasion be difficult to wrap your head spherical. What does a "exceptional tone" endorse? Imagine your self over again speakme to that equal friend approximately the challenge you're masking to your positioned up, however in region of going straight to your keyboard, report your self answering the query out loud. Listen to the recording.

Transcribe the sentences you're especially eager on, then fill in round those strains searching for to match that tone. Once you've written the located up, observe it out loud another time, then skip returned and alternate the places that enjoy awkward or too formal. As you get more snug with the writing way, you'll be able to get that conversational tone right away at the internet page.

Consistency and receive as right with

One of the most important topics is to construct the reader's take shipping of as real with. Make wonderful your content material fabric is normally authentic and actual. If you're making a dependancy of parroting or perhaps outright copying someone else, your weblog is together with no new charge in your reader's lifestyles. Your reviews need to be yours, and also you want to be organized to face with the aid of them. If your readers feel such as you're dependable, they'll be more likely to provide you their unswerving readership.

You can also be dependable to your reader with the resource of posting on a everyday time table and now not missing posts even as you may assist it. Some bloggers publish every day; others put up on pick out days of the week. Twice in line with week is a outstanding frequency at the same time as you're certainly starting out. You're posting often sufficient to offer people a cause to maintain coming again, however you still have time for the alternative factors of your blog, like finding advertisers and talking collectively with your readers, without making you sense crushed.

Blogging fulfillment story: Hero Brown

Hero Brown is the founding father of MuddyStilettos.Co.Uk, "The Urban Guide to the Countryside" for rural regions in England. Brown commenced the weblog as a interest in 2011 when she moved to rural Buckinghamshire and couldn't locate any pinnacle facts at the region. By 2013, it had end up her full-time challenge, with 5,000 subscribers, 6,500 enthusiasts on Facebook and Twitter, and 15,000 unique readers each month.

Brown's ancient past modified into in magazine improving, and he or she or he brings that into her personal style on the net web page. In an interview with Forbes contributor Hester Lacey, Brown stated of her blog, "I consider Muddy Stilettos as a web magazine. It's properly-researched, nicely-written and I'm constantly considering my readers. Lots of blogs by using their nature are a kind of flow into of recognition. I came at it more from a bit of writing attitude."

Brown is likewise very devoted to being honest for her readers, in particular in whom she chooses to have as advertisers on her internet site on-line. "I can also moreover want to earn extra cash from advertising if I modified into a high-quality deal lots much less fussy," Brown says later in that interview, "however if I don't hold that superb bar, the whole purpose for analyzing Muddy Stilettos disappears." By thinking about her target market and retaining their wishes in thoughts, Brown has made a very a success product with Muddy Stilettos that exquisite continues to expand.

Chapter 6: Growing your readership

Having an established readership is the nice manner to draw hobby from advertisers. The broader your target market, the much more likely you may be to get advert clicks or to promote products that each you or your pals have up in the marketplace on their website on line.

The real length of your audience will probable depend plenty for your location of hobby. Blogs in more specialized niches will will be predisposed to have a smaller however greater devoted following than the ones in fields that generate pretty a few well-known hobby.

In fact, at the same time as the place of interest you've decided on will can help you to guess what your aim market should probable seem like, you acquired't without a doubt recognize your readership till you've got got them. Most running a blog interfaces will come up with quite first-rate records on how regularly your pages are considered, and the manner the various ones net internet page views are "precise" (meaning visits from a exceptional traveler) or what number of are repeat visits. Check on those facts periodically.

What style of the placed up appears to get the maximum perspectives? Do your readers like posts that are picture-heavy or text heavy? How prolonged are your maximum-taken into consideration posts? Using this statistics will can help you to refine future content material fabric, tailoring it to what your goal marketplace needs. The extra rate your reader receives from your posts, the much more likely they'll be to hyperlink to them and percent them with exceptional human beings, and the higher chance you have got have been given of growing your subscriber base.

Have a communique together along with your readers

We noted a conversational tone in bankruptcy five, and that's in reality important, but it's equally crucial to interact your readers in real verbal exchange. Always reply to any remarks left to your blog posts, so your readers apprehend that you're listening and inquisitive about what they have to say.

You can also have interaction them in communique on different social media formats. Set up Twitter and Facebook pages to your weblog that are spoil unfastened any non-public social media payments you've got. Make pleasant you're as energetic on the ones money owed as you are to your blog internet page, and much like with weblog comments, make sure to reply to any Tweets or Facebook feedback from your fans much like you could on the weblog.

Posting frequently and replying to comments enables cement that view in readers' minds of you as being a person they may depend on and need to spend their time studying. One-off web web page visitors can be beneficial, but cultivating a base of dependable readers is the wonderful manner to boom your subscription and web internet web page view numbers, and ultimately the extraordinary manner to growth your profits.

Interactive content material material also can assist engage your readers. The most effective way to do this is to put up polls or surveys now and again as part of your posts. If you run a style blog and put up about the satisfactory-dressed celebrities on the purple carpet at an awards show, you can ask the readers who they idea end up the top notch dressed after you put up your evaluations.

These can be fun techniques to start the conversation and include the readers in your technique. If you have were given the hazard to do an interview with a person on your concern, you can invite the readers to submit questions. Giveaways and contests also are a tremendous way to contain your readership and construct the loyalty up right into a community.

Entice subscribers

When it involves readership groups, your subscribers are an extended manner extra essential than your Twitter fans or your Facebook likes. That is your center business enterprise of readers who can pay attention from you without delay When you create a submit or deliver out an email blast, and the oldsters which can be going to be maximum probably to spend their coins for your merchandise, and the organization you can expect for perspectives of your maximum contemporary posts. Especially even as you're first beginning out, growing your subscriber listing want to be one in every of your top priorities.

One smooth manner to increase your subscribers is to offer an incentive to those who sign on. Blogging professionals name this "improving your price" in a functionality subscriber's eyes; cynics could call this "bribing human beings." Whatever you call it, it's a established, powerful manner to boom subscriptions. The key's to offer an incentive that offers real fee to subscribers with out lowering into your profits margin.

An awesome whitepaper or useful resource may want to make a amazing signal-up incentive because it's something you fine must create as quickly as that still offers readers lengthy-time period rate. If you sell products or services in your net website online online, you can provide a reduction to subscribers, both as a one-time coupon or a lower "subscriber price." Discounts can construct each client loyalty and your backside line. Someone who wouldn't have looked at your keep earlier than may also moreover acquire this if he's were given a discount.

Make it easy for people to join your internet site on-line. Pop-up subscription invites are the present day-day fashion. Some readers will discover them demanding, and a few ad blockading software program software will save you them from beginning, however in addition they'll be powerful at letting readers comprehend you've got were given a mailing list. If you'd as an possibility positioned a hyperlink in your internet web site on-line, make sure it's easy to discover and really visible to most website online traffic—don't cowl it in a menu or at the bottom of the internet page. A new vacationer shouldn't want to search for a way to get updates whilst you post.

If you are taking part in the e-book to this point, please permit me understand.

Blogging achievement story: Alborz Fallah

Alborz Fallah started out out his blog CarAdvice.Com.Au as a element undertaking even as he emerge as although jogging a whole-time undertaking. His is an remarkable story to expose that someone can start a new blog in an oversaturated marketplace (like car compare web sites) and however manage to achieve success through carefully focusing in your target audience.

Rather than looking for to compete with every car blog in the international, Fallah targeted in on running a weblog about motors for fellow Australians. His weblog generated large internet page website online traffic, enough that he had been given buyers interested in his product and has thinking about the reality that save you his day job to attention on the blog entire time.

Fallah started in 2006 as a one-man group on a net site making $10 everyday with day on AdSense. CarAdvice now has a 30-man organization of professionals with test garages and places of work in Sydney, Melbourne, Brisbane, and Perth. The internet web website online receives over 3 hundred,000 unique month-to-month site visitors and makes over $three million in step with one year in income—all because of the truth Fallah understood that he had to purpose the right goal market to gain fulfillment.

Chapter 7: Networking and community

Even if you write in a reasonably restrained location of interest, opportunities are there is probably as a minimum a few other bloggers available writing about your concern recall. In a giant revel in, this is your area of interest's network. The more famous the subject, the larger the community it will likely be, and the smaller sub-organizations will exist inside the essential. In some techniques, you may consider the blogosphere like a excessive college, in which human beings communicate commonly to the people of their clique—and much like in excessive faculty, all the cool children usually generally tend to loaf around collectively.

There are 3 techniques you can method the lifestyles of the community. You can forget about about them and no longer trouble your self with what others are writing. You can take a passive hobby, following them to maintain up with what they're saying however now not interacting with their internet net web page.

Or you may actively have interaction with them, leaving feedback on their posts or linking lower again to them in your private. You don't must interact with distinct bloggers to achieve success, however being energetic in the network is one way to help expand your readership greater speedy.

You moreover don't should limit yourself to interacting with bloggers to your field. Become an lively reader and follower of any blogs you enjoy, notwithstanding the truth that they're no longer generally associated with your personal. At the very least, specific readers who discover your remarks to be insightful may additionally check out your blog and locate it exciting.

Making pals with unique bloggers and net net web page proprietors will assist you to generate greater website online site traffic through getting your call out in extra places. The greater a weblog put up is connected to and visited, the more it is going to show up in

Google searches, which in flip will carry you even extra net web site web page site visitors.

Remember that every time you're posting a comment on a person else's weblog, the remark need to be by way of and massive about them, and actually minimally (or never) about you. Link decrease lower back to your very own weblog only if it's legitimately applicable to the undertaking of the put up. Spamming human beings's remark sections with advertisements in your blog will now not make you any friends, and could not land you as many readers within the lengthy-time period as in case you come to be appeared for leaving witty, insightful, or beneficial comments.

You may in all likelihood experience anonymous at the same time as you're interacting with humans at the net, however you need to additionally don't forget that it's an area wherein reputation is the whole lot and statistics can spread very an extended way, in no time. Be as type, courteous, and well mannered for your online interactions as you may be with humans face to face. Remember that the entirety you do on line associated with your weblog is a reflected photo of your brand. A lively debate in a commentary section can get interest from capacity readers, however commonly be respectful of various bloggers, even whilst you disagree.

Face to stand networking

One of the bizarre things approximately strolling a weblog as a profession is that even in case your posts acquire 10,000 human beings every day, it's feasible you'll in no way physical have interaction with any of them. Attending networking sports and conferences can remind you that there are faces and people inside the again of each placed up and commentary.

There are seminars and workshops geared inside the course of bloggers. These can truly be beneficial in that you may meet special bloggers and research from their evaluations, but they're not the remarkable region to meet your fans, too. Attending occasions or meetings associated with your area of hobby can provide remarkable networking opportunities each with exceptional bloggers and your capability readership. If you weblog approximately films, attend a network comedian con.

For bloggers in tech fields, exchange shows can be first-rate places to peer the cutting-edge-day enhancements and meet fellow lovers. You can quite a wonderful deal guarantee a number of the alternative attendees could be bloggers to your discipline, and even on the off threat you don't make any networking connections, you'll studies some element from the event to percent alongside aspect your readers.

Blogger achievement story: Michael Dunlop

The creator of IncomeDiary.Com has been developing a residing on the internet from the time he changed right into a teen and at 21 has already come to be a prominent discern in the on foot a weblog international. In a bit of writing on his internet web page entitled "The True Story of my Overnight Success," Dunlop talks about an internet layout internet site he ran in advance than beginning Income Diary, referred to as ShoutGFX. He have been given the idea for the internet page from every special famous layout internet site and concept he may additionally want to advantage from a similar model. He took numerous individuals of the unique discussion board with him to his new web page.

ShoutGFX in the long run modified into added down at the same time as humans did the same issue, beginning their personal commercial enterprise primarily based mostly on Dunlop's idea. Though his corporation moreover suffered from awful coding (an illustration of a few unique point: almost about outsourcing art work, you regularly get what you pay for), the final lesson Dunlop took away have end up that "what goes spherical comes spherical." Kindness repays the kindness, however if you're underhanded, you'll appeal to others of a like mind.

Dunlop goes on within the article to talk approximately one among the biggest keys to his achievement: seeing his screw ups as gaining knowledge of reports in place of crushing defeats. If you want to expand your emblem, you on occasion will have to take risks and check with new topics. Some of them will workout; a number of them acquired't. If you research from it, despite the fact that, no revel in is ever wasted. Rather than give up on the equal time as he confronted setbacks, Dunlop persisted to push in advance and now earns a six-figure earnings as an entire-time blogger.

Maximizing Profit

There are three most vital ways that bloggers make cash: advertising income (cash advertisers pay you for region for your internet site), associate income (rate obtained from some different business enterprise once they promote a product via your internet web site), or a right away sale (reader charge to you for a services or products provided for your internet net web page).

Advertising and partner income are passive earnings sources. This is not to mention you have not any manipulate over the earnings; you may use page positioning and content material fabric to maximise viewer clicks, and may manage which advertisers carry out in your page, however you aren't right now liable for the product. These are the right and maximum not unusual assets of earnings for bloggers, but require you to get a large amount of internet site web site site visitors to generate valid earnings.

Direct profits can take masses of superb paperwork. In a right away sale, you are answerable for turning in a product to the reader. Direct income can be some element which you make and deliver to them, an eBook or PDF that's despatched to their inbox as quick as they purchase it, or a membership to a talk board or list that contributors pay for on a month-to-month or each year basis.

A photo clothier or photographer may also use their weblog at the facet of a freelancing commercial enterprise corporation, the usage of the blog as a platform to gain new clients. It can also be your services as an employer expert and blogger which can be up available on the market. Paid speaking engagements, consultations, or commands and workshops are all income streams below the direct sale umbrella that many a success bloggers use to growth their income.

Chapter 8: Advertising

Most people who set out looking for to put in writing a weblog to make coins—in desire to people who start as hobbyists and turn into companies—achieve this imagining they'll make all their cash via advertising. Just write some posts, toss some banner commercials on there, and you've had been given yourself a coins cow. Right?

Well, no longer quite. The primary thing you need to make coins from advertising and marketing and marketing and advertising and marketing is lots of site visitors, and for a fledgling weblog with most effective a handful of internet internet web page perspectives consistent with day, you're now not going to discover too many those who want to pay you money for location for your web web page. A right rule of thumb is to get at the least 10,000 net page perspectives consistent with month (that's among 3 hundred and four hundred views a day) in advance than you go out searching out advertisers.

Larger ad networks and groups can also moreover want net websites to reveal 20,000 or possibly 100,000 views consistent with month before they'll be inquisitive about securing advertising and advertising and advertising area. While the exact numbers advertisers are seeking out will rely upon your region of interest, 10,000 views a month is a splendid baseline reason to set for yourself in case you'd like advertising and advertising and marketing to function considered one of your profits streams.

Google AdSense

The biggest advert community for blogs and other web sites currently at the internet is Google AdSense. It's the only that many new bloggers flip to because it has an open reputation coverage with reference to definitely one among a kind niches and site site visitors degrees. A slower blog will make a great deal a lot less coins than a immoderate-website traffic net internet web page, of path, and there are some ad formats which are handiest available to people with better viewership counts.

AdSense is simple to use in assessment to maximum advert networks. The turn component of this ease, of path, is that Google takes a reduce of the advertiser's cash as a commission for offering the advert provider—approximately 32% of what the advertiser can pay regular with click on goes straight away to Google.

The precise quantity that you may make the use of Google AdSense varies relying on what duration and style of ad you use, what vicinity of hobby your blog is in, and what sort of website online site visitors you get. There are 3 excellent bid fashions that advertisers can use to pay for the space on your web page. The charge-in line with-click on on model is the most not unusual. In this model, you get a charge on every occasion a tourist clicks at the advert, however the fact that they don't skip any similarly via the web page.

There's additionally a price consistent with thousand impressions version, in which you receives a rate regular with thousand ad views, irrespective of the truth that the site visitors don't interact with the ad. The zero.33 type is the charge consistent with engagement version, wherein the advertiser can pay you for whenever a viewer completes a selected venture, like looking a video or finishing a survey.

Knowing all of that is valuable in gaining greater insight into how AdSense works, however one drawback of the usage of AdSense over more selective ad networks is which you don't get to govern which sort of ad is going to your internet web page. Google determines which one will paintings great given your area of hobby and your website web site traffic ranges.

Since they're on foot on charge, they've got a quite wonderful incentive to select the fashion and content that's going to make you the maximum money, however in the long run it's as a whole lot as Google who advertises on your website online and the usage of what format. You manipulate the dimensions and placement of the ad, however that's approximately it.

Because it's so smooth to use (and generates severa earnings in the proper times) Google AdSense is often the way to move if you have spherical 10,000 net internet web page perspectives consistent with month and are just starting to paintings with advertising and advertising as an earnings flow into.

Other advertising and marketing and advertising and marketing networks

There are a plethora of diverse ad networks to be had for bloggers, most of so that you can ask for a higher minimal site traffic than Google AdSense. Some are quite selective (Revcontent is understood for being hard to sign up for and rejects ninety eight% of applicants). There are some that don't require a minimal site visitors wide variety to apply, making them maximum beneficial for ultra-current bloggers.

Among the ones are BidVertiser, Clicksor, and BlogAds. Do a few research before signing up with a modern-day-day advert community. Check out internet websites that use it to see the manner it shows up on their pages, and if you could speak to special bloggers approximately their enjoy with the internet web page, that's even higher.

Keep in mind that the greater one-of-a-kind advert networks have limited get right of entry to for a reason. Their advertisers are probably to pay extra cash in exchange for a guarantee of higher viewership. As your website site visitors grows, considering large advert networks can be a superb manner to growth your profits.

Direct advertisers

Ad networks run on a middle-guy earnings version. They do the art work of finding advertisers and arranging price, and in alternate, they take a percent of the cash for themselves. Communicating straight away with an advertiser method you get to keep all the coins, but it additionally method you want to deal right now with the companies and negotiate expenses and phrases.

Direct advertisers are generally a overdue-degree addition to a blogger's earnings streams because of the fact maximum direct advertisers will need to peer higher web web page site visitors numbers than ad networks in advance than committing. It also calls on the way to be a bit greater business enterprise savvy than signing up for an advert community.

One situation wherein direct advertising and marketing should artwork for a decrease traffic weblog is if you run a internet site aimed towards a town or community. A small industrial corporation owner might possibly discover it in reality nicely really worth his even as to promote it on a blog that best receives 5,000 internet web page perspectives according to month if all five,000 of those perspectives are probable to be from functionality customers. While direct advertisements will be predisposed to be employed through installed blogs, don't rule the idea out if a capability opportunity comes alongside. Affiliate earnings

Affiliate income is even as you earn a price through way of promoting someone else's merchandise in your website. It's similar to marketing in that it's a passive income flow into, and also you don't want to supply gadgets or offerings, however in comparison to advertising and marketing and marketing, you simplest get the earnings if your affiliate makes a sale. Though excessive-site site visitors web sites are much more likely to earn coins thru an associate software, accomplice earnings may be more worthwhile for a weblog because it's building web page visitors than advertising profits because it doesn't rely strictly on website online-view numbers.

Amazon's affiliate software software is the splendid-acknowledged and is probably the pleasant place to start. It's clean to sign up for, and the net site on-line has this sort of brilliant array of merchandise in the marketplace that you're very probably to discover some element that relates to your region of interest. Though you may cope with associate hyperlinks like advertising and marketing and motive them to a passive element of your internet page, associate products are more likely to sell if you take a look at them or promote them with an actual positioned up.

Though you don't get to control who advertises for your internet website on line through an ad network, you do get to govern which merchandise you promote thru an associate software. You should only recommend merchandise that you believe might be beneficial to your readers if you want to keep their believe and loyalty. You want to also make certain that the product connects logically to your preferred niche.

Improving your ad sales

As smooth as it would sound, in which you location the classified ads on a web page can effect your readers' degree of engagement with it and in the end with how an lousy lot money you could make from it. While banner commercials at the top of the internet page are one of the extra not unusual marketing and advertising and advertising styles, this isn't constantly the fantastic area to position the ad to get reader interaction. Including the advert inside the foremost location of your posts will increase your average clicks consistent with go to.

While you could not understand the businesses that advertise on your net web site on line at the same time as you're the usage of an ad community, in case you be a part of up advertisers straight away you want to assist them whenever viable. This doesn't necessarily advocate writing "advertorials" (posts in particular committed to promoting advertisers) until doing so could feel natural and herbal for your blog, but you can interact with them in one-of-a-kind strategies with out diminishing the integrity of your internet internet page.

Tweet in your advertisers now and again. Know what they're as a good deal as and in the occasion that they're liberating a latest product or have an upcoming occasion that your readers should gain from knowing about, make certain to share that records. Anything you could do to growth your fee from the advertiser's mindset will fine assist you to bring in extra sales.

Blogger fulfillment story: Daniel Scocco

Daniel Scocco is extraordinary-seemed for walking the internet web site on-line DailyBlogTips.Com. At this element, Scocco is more targeted on his software program program software business enterprise and his online advertising and marketing and advertising schooling path, in area of overseeing the every day workings of his blog. Though he does a number of the writing himself, he additionally employs a personnel of paid writers and brings other bloggers in for tourist posts.

He's grown his weblog to the factor that it generates a massive quantity of passive earnings for him, letting him attention on his unique profits streams. In a contemporary year, Scocco became capable of make spherical $a hundred,000 from Google AdSense by myself, proving it's possible to make a residing income using AdSense—if you're inclined to put in the artwork to assemble the web page.

Chapter 9: Diversifying your earnings

As changed into said inside the starting segment, strolling a weblog may be very now not regularly a stand-on my own corporation. Even if it starts offevolved offevolved out that way, most bloggers discover they may be able to construct their earnings greater speedy through manner of diversifying their profits streams than in the event that they labored off of advertising and marketing and associate income from their blog by myself. Manage your expansions carefully.

Experimentation is the fine manner to develop your enterprise agency, but perform a bit pre-planning to ensure you'll be able to hold the identical amazing on every your weblog and for your new challenge earlier than you decide to it. In some instances, you can locate it in the long run more valuable to outsource some of the paintings or bring about a paid creator or assistant to ensure which you're able to juggle all the factors of your organisation.

Any new income motion you add for your weblog need to complement it. Remember that precise work consequences in suitable opportunities and that popularity is beneficial on your prolonged-time period achievement. It can also moreover serve you better to do matters specially than 5 topics which may be best of mediocre excellent.

Especially in case you're going into the arena of product profits, handing over a low-first-rate product, taking a long term to supply gadgets, or having terrible customer service can become using readers away in vicinity of supporting to beautify your logo. Strike a balance: you need to be inclined to test and take risks, but must despite the fact that take some time to think via and plan new ventures, in order that they have got the first-rate chance to collect success.

Your industrial company will change as it grows and progresses. Things that labored well for you at the same time as you have got been first beginning out might have much less of an effect to your backside line as you expand; functionality income assets which may be useless or too volatile in an early degree of your weblog also can emerge as feasible when you've superior a following. Again, stability is top. Find the topics that provide you with the outcomes you need and keep to do them, however in no manner prevent seeking out topics that could work better.

Potential income streams

The possibilities for monetizing your weblog are actually infinite, and while a few strategies have tested effective for others, no listing of profits streams can be sincerely entire. Don't rule a few aspect out definitely due to the truth you don't see all people else talking approximately it, however in case you're looking for strategies to increase your income out of your blogs, keep in mind one of the following alternatives.

Member internet web sites

A paid segment of your web web web page can be an fantastic way to provide more rate in your readers at the same time as expanding your earnings streams, and may be useful for a weblog in a smaller area of interest, whose readership is of the small, committed variety. The caveat to this is which you want to ensure that a paid member web website online is honestly supplying a significant boom in fee over your loose content material, otherwise you'll danger leaving your maximum committed readers feeling ripped off.

There are many types of member-high-quality internet web sites. Forums and directories are well-known codecs. Carol Tice (who writes the blog Make a Living Writing) brought a paid phase to her internet page called The Writer's Den that offers one-on-one education and other services for aspiring freelancers, like a way board and boot camps. Since her internet website on line facilitates freelancers make a residing, it modified right into a logical and organic extension of her logo.

While a member's best website on line doesn't require you to make any bodily products, it's going to moreover require greater complicated coding than your conventional weblog web web page. Unless you've have been given a heritage in programming or improvement, you can want to lease someone to help you set it up. Make nice to plot sufficient time and money to outsource the ones projects on the same time as you're thinking about whether or not or now not or not to try them.

EBooks

The most a success eBooks come from bloggers whose brand is primarily based on expertise. You can each launch the eBook as a PDF right away from your website or via a shop like Amazon for almost no financial investment. It is a time investment to launch an eBook. You need to make sure it includes new cloth that's now not exceptional a re-hash of the statistics readers can get for your weblog without cost. An powerful eBook scenario depend is probably an in-depth assessment of a style for your trouble or a whole how-to reply of a commonplace hassle.

Income from an eBook has a dishonest to accumulate its highest ranges shortly after its preliminary launch. Referencing the book in your destiny posts or strolling a promoting must reason spikes in profits, but in case you're advertising the ebook, proper the bulk of your subscribers will buy it proper off the bat in the occasion that they're going to. Subsequent spikes in profits have a propensity to be from new readers who've come to you because the initial launch.

Online publications

Online publications can take many bureaucracy for a blogger. The only way to make a direction is to install writing it as a sequence of PDF documents that your reader purchases and research on their very own— very just like an eBook, but with bodily games and further assets designed in particular to train the reader.

Recording media to accompany the direction may want to make it revel in more personal and gives the direction extra rate. Whether you do it as an audio report or a video, those who buy the elegance will benefit from listening to you offer an motive in the back of the ideas out loud. Video may be particularly useful for physical or visible niches, like fitness or design, wherein demonstrating the idea may be a lot less complicated than explaining it.

The most time-massive route style is to meet with the students in actual time through a talk room or on-line training portal. Real-time courses can be the first-rate layout for delivered superior requirements, wherein the readers may additionally have an entire lot of questions which might be hard to reply in a ebook, or for workshop-fashion publications, designed to help the readers observed from each one of a kind similarly to from you. The drawback of this fashion of sophistication is that it calls for human beings to be to be had at a specific time to attend, which can also restriction hobby and attendance.

Workshops and seminars

The same fabric that you train in an internet route may be positioned to use in an in-character workshop or seminar. You may also want to gift this at an employer convention or set up an independent seminar on your location. The gain of an in-man or woman lecture or seminar is that it lets in your enthusiasts to meet and have interaction with you, if you need to growth their feeling of loyalty. The disadvantage of seminars is they will be expensive to put on, in particular in comparison to the advantage and performance of an internet direction.

Blogging success tale: Darren Rowse

Darren Rowse is the founder and editor of ProBlogger Blog Tips and Digital Photography School. Not simplest has he had incredible fulfillment of his very very very own, but his blog is likewise one of the excellent assets on the net for different bloggers looking for recommendation. In a 2013 submit on ProBlogger, Rowse cited the 12 extremely good income streams he has developed. His weblog commenced out as a hobby however have been given well-known sufficient he experimented with AdSense and the Amazon Affiliate Program after the primary yr.

Starting from the ones humble origins, he extended his logo to consist of speaking engagements, books, and a consulting organisation. ProBlogger now abilties a interest board and a member web web page, every of which contribute everyday revenue.

This boom of his emblem befell over the direction of a decade. Rowse took risks and wasn't afraid to address new responsibilities, but additionally managed his enlargement cautiously. During the object on his revenue streams published on ProBlogger, Rowse says, "The key's to pick out out some thing to attempt to see whether or not or not it connects collectively with your readership and to investigate as lots as you can whilst you're doing it." It's absolutely really worth noting he no longer offers the consulting business enterprise.

Being willing to dispose of profits streams that aren't generating can be as important as including new ones which can be.

Chapter 10: Marketing your blog

You don't want a huge advertising and marketing and advertising and marketing and advertising rate range to raise your weblog's visitors upwards of 10,000 perspectives a month and to get identified inner your area of hobby. We already noted a few techniques to construct readership back in chapter 6, however how can you trap even extra human beings for your internet web page?

Facebook and Twitter are in reality particular places to begin. Don't restrict your advertising and marketing to asking your pals and own family to love your business agency internet web page. Facebook commercials are very less high-priced and can be targeted to best readers or companies. Follow exceptional bloggers to your area of interest on Twitter.

You can also get a follow decrease again, and even if not, they'll have interesting topics to mention. It's advice that bears repeating: turning into a member of the conversation on your network is one of the high-quality ways you may permit humans recognise you exist.

Team up with small agencies

In financial ruin eight, I stated getting direct ad sales from small companies, however you could moreover shape more symbiotic relationships with small businesses to assist each of you increase your manufacturers. Writing evaluations of their products which may be then shared on their internet site will deliver greater links and location visitors lower again to you on the identical time it lets in them to promote their merchandise.

Remember that maximum small business enterprise owners are similar to you—they're trying to get as a excellent deal exposure as feasible even as no longer having to spend a ton of more money.

Sponsor or host activities

If you run a weblog about biking, you could emerge as a sponsor for a network motorbike race. If you run a weblog about famous tradition, you can host an Oscar viewing birthday celebration at a neighborhood bar or eating place and live Tweet or chat together together with your enthusiasts.

We have a tendency no longer to consider inman or woman sports activities as being beneficial for a blogger due to the fact our target market is on-line and can come from any nook of the globe, but don't forget about about that your area is entire of capability readers, even if your area of hobby isn't in particular dedicated on your metropolis.

Contests

Saveur.Com honors the first-rate foodie blogs in numerous training at the stop of every yr. WriteToDone.Com ranks the pinnacle blogs for writers. For each niche, there may be someone out there ready to recognize the bloggers in the concern. Winning an award can be a first rate way to gain publicity. Some you may enter or get nominated for, and others are primarily based totally on reader votes, so test out what's happening in your niche and recollect how you can placed yourself in an first-rate location to compete.

Be charitable

It feels precise to offer returned—and from a branding perspective, it's a high-quality recognition decorate and a hazard to gain visibility while doing some thing precise. Charity doesn't need to signify giving cash to someone, both—in fact, the first-class possibilities encompass donating it sluggish or weblog vicinity to a reason.

A fitness blogger might possibly ask readers to sponsor them in a most cancers walk, as an example, on the same time as a monetary blogger would probably placed on a series of free workshops for people in a close-by library or community center to help them better preserve their financial health. Giving lower back to your readers and the network can installation your call and your brand inside the minds of latest capability enthusiasts.

Blogging success tale: John Resig

John Resig positioned TheChive.Com collectively alongside along with his brother Leo in 2008. Described by way of way of Bloomberg Business as "a crowdsourced, Internet version of a lad mag—the Maxim of the 21st century," through using manner of 2013 The Chive had grown proper proper into a tremendously well-known net website with 20.1 million particular web site visitors in line with month. Though it would appear atypical for a internet site based totally mostly on humorous photos and lovely girls, the Chive owes plenty of its growth and achievement to its severa charitable tasks.

Chive readers have raised hundreds of loads of bucks thru Chive Charities that has lengthy beyond to wounded veterans and unwell or underprivileged kids across the usa of a. As Resig stated in his interview with Bloomberg Business, the net internet website "moved from a internet web site to a emblem to way of life", one which's a weird but a fulfillment stability of frat house surroundings and random acts of kindness.

How has The Chive controlled to expand this kind of a success emblem so rapid? They targeted on constructing their audience instead of their earnings margin and then capitalized on their dependable fan base via manner of way of promoting branded merchandise and website hosting meet-america of americaacross the united states.

One person stated of the net web page, "If I see a person in a Chive T-shirt, I understand what shape of person they may be and that I'll probably get together with them." If you could cultivate that kind of response out of your fan base, you may do not forget your weblog very a hit definitely.

Chapter 11: Types of Blogging Platforms

Now that you recognize that you may make money from strolling a blog, the subsequent step is to pick out the right on foot a blog platform. This choice may be a little confusing to make, in particular thinking about there are loads of alternatives right now in 2019. Blogging systems have come an prolonged manner, and there are unique kinds of blogs catered to the distinctive goals and capabilities for every blogger available. In this economic wreck, we are able to have a study the outstanding (FREE!) jogging a weblog systems that you could earn coins from. We look at loose structures due to the reality all systems are simply loose to sign up for up and use at its primary diploma, or at the least free for an ordeal duration.

Once you start exploring and the use of its functions, trying out to look if this is some thing that works for you, you may get a remarkable revel in of the manner topics may be appropriate to your jogging a blog capabilities. Let's get into discussing the professionals and cons of every of them. Firstly, proper here is the list of blogs we're capable of be looking at:

- WordPress.Org

- WordPress.Com

- Blogger

- Wix

- Tumblr

- Medium

- Joomla

- Weebly

What is a walking a weblog platform?

A on foot a weblog platform is essentially a place or a domain in which you can create an perform your weblog internet site. A strolling a weblog software software or company, but, is wherein you can post your articles from- it is essentially a content fabric fabric manage system or CMS. In simpler terms, a software software utility platform that permits you to create your blog publish without any form of programming or coding information is a going for walks a weblog platform. As noted previously, there are masses of blogging structures available, but you want a few factor that suits no longer nice your desires however moreover a few problem this is widely used round the world. Here is a listing of the location's most used blogging platform:

- WordPress.Org - 48%

- Blogger- 25%

- WordPress.Com - 13%

- Drupal- 3%

- Joomla- 2%

- Wix- 1%

- Tumblr- 1%

- Medium- 1%

- Weebly- 1%

The Best Free Blogging Platforms to Make Money

It is important to pick a strolling a blog platform this is famous as you may get masses of guidelines, hints, plug-ins, situation subjects, and solutions from all around the internet. Also, famous blogging systems adventure immoderate on are looking for engine effects.

●WordPress.Org

WordPress.Org is some of the incredible blogging structures available, not excellent in 2019 however ever due to the fact that blogs commenced becoming commonplace in the net location. At present, WordPress currently hosts extra than 33% of net sites on the internet. The motive for this is because of the truth WordPress.Org is reasonably smooth to use. Apart from that, it moreover has a totally useful and active individual community that has loads of statistics, tips, and the way-tos. WordPress.Org, a self-hosted walking a weblog platform, and open-deliver software program software.

The Pros:

•You are on one of the most importantly used famous loose strolling a blog systems in the international

•You get to construct quite lots any shape of net internet site you want

•There are lots of unfastened and top elegance topics you could choose from on your website online format

•Access to approximately fifty four,000 loose plugins to customize and enhance your website on-line

• It is extremely search engine optimization fine

• It is likewise made to be cell-responsive

• You get high performance with immoderate safety

• You also have get proper of access to to gadget that you can extend your problem remember range to fit you

• The editor uses a Gutenberg block

The Cons

• As WordPress.Org is a self-hosted jogging a blog platform, you want if you need to control your weblog in your non-public, and this consists of backing it up and installing extra safety.

The Cost

WordPress.Org is unfastened to use, but you moreover can also want a web web hosting agency that you could set up and start constructing your blog. Plus, a internet site call is also surprisingly critical. Hosting is pretty popular, and it generally begins offevolved approximately $3.Ninety 5 a month, depending on the issuer you choose. Bluehost or SiteGround is one of the quality places to start as a novice. Both of those internet hosting vendors are recommended with WordPress.Org, and in addition they installed a unfastened vicinity in addition to an SSL certificates without price. You truly have a preference of buying your personal area call in addition to net web hosting organization, and in case you do this, then your great choice is to go with WordPress.Org running a weblog platform.

●WordPress.Com

WordPress.Com and WordPress.Org are definitely one of a type systems for taking walks a weblog. This is a few detail you want to understand about the early on-set. So what's the difference? With WordPress.Org, the CMS is in which you get to expand or host your very very own blog with a hosting service employer. With WordPress.Com, it is similar to other unfastened running a blog structures in that you get to create your personal blog using their website online. Plenty of novices choose to begin their running a blog with WordPress.Com due to its ease-of-use. Blogging is unfastened with WordPress.Com, however if you want their pinnacle magnificence services and your very personal custom area call, you then definitely definately moreover need to pay top elegance fees as well.

●The Pros:

●You do not need any shape of setup

●It is easy to use and manipulate your weblog

●You can use the cellular and pc apps to replace your blog web page from anywhere

●You very very own the content material fabric material in your internet site because of this you could switch it whenever, anywhere

•You moreover get free Jetpack essential abilties

•You additionally get 3GB garage region

The Cons

•You have confined options for personalization

•You moreover can't run your personal advertisements

•WordPress.Com does now not will let you sync Google AdSense

•You can earn cash thru WordAds

•Your account can be closed at any 2d in case you violate their terms and situations

The Cost

The number one WordPress.Com internet website on line is unfastened, but you moreover mght become with WordPress's very private advertising and marketing and advertising and banners. However, in case you pay for their top elegance services, you could have your very personal area and eliminate their branding Ads. Their pinnacle rate costs are $eight a month whereas their company fee is at $25 a month.

●Blogger

Blogger is every specific famous desire and a sensible one to weblog and to make money. It moreover has a huge series of subjects that you could use absolutely unfastened to your weblog. It is likewise called one of the great blogs for novices. Just much like the WordPress blogs, Blogger is free, but if you want their top beauty services, then you definitely need to pay. For bloggers who use Blogger, your area address might be yourname.Blogspot.Com, however in case you pay for a custom place call, then you get to customise your location. This is the right platform for beginners, whether or now not you want to apply it as a non-public weblog or a business blog.

You can put in your commercial so long as you're prison for Google AdSense even in case you are on a unfastened plan. This is one of the quality free walking a blog structures if you need to make cash the use of Google AdSense.

The Pros

•Blogger is a loose taking walks a weblog platform

•It is also clean to apply and clean to manage the net website online on line- you do no longer need coding understanding

•You can use Google Adsense in this weblog to earn coins

The Cons

•You have limited options to develop your weblog

•You do no longer have access to plugins or extensions to decorate your weblog's functionality

•While there are masses of problems, it isn't always as varied as the ones on WordPress

•You run the chance of your account final at any time if you violate their terms and situations

•As you develop and start making a residing, you may want to make bigger your net internet site on line, but you'd locate that it is restricted

The Cost

The Blogger account is free; however, it comes with limited alternatives. You want to pay top beauty costs to have your very personal custom domain name. If the usage of Google AdSense is your number one reason to your weblog, then Blogger is the manner to go.

•Wix

Wix is an upgraded platform within the global of blogging. Wix started out as an easy-to-use jogging a blog and internet site possibility in case you want to create a free blog or net web web page. You can use this like each other weblog or internet web page really free, however like all the specific options, you need pinnacle rate plans for a custom place. Wix does not will let you located your very personal commercials in at the same time as you are on their unfastened plan however it does offer you loads more capabilities of creating a full-fledged internet site with plugins and state of affairs subjects to make it professional so long as your imagination is going.

The Pros

●Wix is extraordinarily smooth to set up

●It is a great opportunity if you are looking to create a net website online with none coding information

●It's drag and drop elements allow you to construct your internet internet web page with out troubles the usage of the Wix Editor

●It is also mobile optimized and search engine advertising exceptional

•Wix moreover has dynamic pages because of this you can create the equal unmarried format for one hundred pages

The Cons

•Its free account has confined alternatives

•Wix shows their commercials on your internet internet web site

•You nice have one hazard to select a template for your website, and you cannot trade it

•Wix does no longer provide distinct 0.33 birthday celebration apps

•Their e-alternate alternatives are restricted

•It isn't always an wonderful choice to make cash, however it's miles a extremely good opportunity for a internet web page

The Cost

Their maximum essential plan is at $5 a month, however it comes with the Wix emblem ads and confined bandwidth. If you choose the $14 a month, then you honestly have their endless plan. Their VIP plan is at $29 a month.

•Tumblr

The global's maximum well-known microblogging internet site and social networking internet site. This internet site permits you to make the strolling a blog enjoy terrific from the rest. Tumblr's community can be very unique from that of the alternative blogs with its community more into fandom, GIFs, bordering to eroticism, and masses of anime. Tumblr additionally allows you to apply Google AdSense if you have a custom region name, however it does no longer permit you to mounted your very very personal ad whilst you're the opposite on that jogging a weblog platform.

The Pros

•Tumblr is easy to use and loose

•It furthermore has blanketed social networking into the aggregate

•It permits you to position up multimedia from films to GIFs in a short-term weblog

The Cons

•Tumblr has very particular capabilities to allow it to be a microblogging net website online so if you want to extend your blog; you want to transport a few region else except you're happy with its microblogging competencies

•The lack of plugins makes it difficult to feature in any additional capabilities

•It is tough to replace or export content material from platform to a few exclusive ought to making a decision to move a ways from Tumblr and cross at once to some thing like WordPress

The Cost

Tumblr is unfastened just like the different structures, but you want to pay for a custom domain call for your blog. You additionally want to pay for 0.33 celebration apps if you want to use it on your blog.

●Medium

Medium is a very well-known publishing jogging a blog platform that caters particularly to prolonged-form writing, with a gap goal market of writers, reporters as well as tale writers. Medium is free to use as properly, however for readers, they could need to pay to observe articles as there may be a club rate. You cannot hooked up your very very own classified ads except, like Tumblr, you have got your very own custom area. Medium is the prolonged-form version of Tumblr, and it's far a extremely good platform to apply if being profitable thru writing articles is your cause.

To come to be a Medium member, your price starts at $5 a month, and it could bypass as an awful lot as $50 a 12 months, but the super thing is you get endless get proper of entry to to the net's quality writers, and you'd furthermore get mind that you can not get anywhere else.

Medium expenses a membership fee to support its writers the identical way Patreon prices its individuals to guide its artists and revolutionary network. The club charge is sent among writers based totally on how attractive their content fabric is with their intention market.

The Pros

●Medium is pretty clean to set up and use. In fact, there may be little to no setup required

●It has an clean to cope with interface

●It is likewise unfastened to apply

The Cons

●The platform's features are restricted

●You are not capable of run your very own commercials in case you use the platform freed from price

•If you misplaced your Medium account, you lose your fanatics

The Cost

As with all the systems above, if you want custom capabilities and upgrades, you want to pay for it. It is quite preferred.

•Joomla

This platform stocks similar functions to WordPress.Org. It is likewise open-deliver, and it has its very private Content Management System. It is a platform used typically with the aid of the usage of way of non-income, small businesses as well as large agencies counting on what their goals are. As of 2019, Joomla has over 2 million lively net web websites. Like WordPress, Joomla moreover has extensions and plugins, and it is also a free blogging platform. You can also run your non-public commercials in this platform which furthermore method that this is some different platform that makes it easy to make coins via running a blog.

The Pros

●You can artwork on an open-supply software program application

●You have a are looking for engine optimized out of the container

●They additionally have extremely good format skills and functionalities

●Pretty right safety

●An extremely good choice for incomes profits

The Cons

●As it's miles similar to WordPress.Org, you'd be difficult-pressed to location your finger on which one is better- making this preference can be difficult

●You need to control your personal blog and net internet web site further the manner you will with WP.Org

•Joomla's community is lots smaller than that of WordPress due to this that restricted help and limited development

The Cost

You want a dependable website hosting company to host your going for walks a weblog platform. Charges are approximately the same with WordPress.

•Weebly

Not to be burdened with Weibo, that is some one-of-a-kind free running a blog platform that is more of a weblog internet site builder. It is one of the splendid systems to apply in case you want to assemble a web save. You may also even need a top class plan if you want to run an eCommerce agency. For Weebly's buying card feature to be brought, you need to enhance your plan to a Pro plan or a Business plan. They have the easy SSL protection, and it furthermore comes with 500MB of information garage. On the turn facet, it has a subdomain, so if you need to have your very very personal custom domain identification, then you should, of route, want to go pinnacle magnificence.

The Pros

●It's an smooth setup with clean drag and drop capabilities and interface

●You have masses of free strolling a blog templates to pick out out from

●It is seek engine advertising and advertising optimized

●You do no longer want any coding knowledge

●The protection is minimal

●There are masses of media and third birthday celebration integration alternatives whilst you need to increase the weblog's capability

The Cons

●If you're at the loose plan, the capabilities are of route limited

- Since its media integration is strong, you will possibly grow to be going for walks into restricted region the more media you add

- You are unable to run your personal advertisements to make coins. Instead, their classified ads may be introduced for your internet site online

- There isn't any cellphone assist given to basic plans

- Migrating statistics and content material material from this weblog to every other is hard

The Cost

The seasoned plan is available in at $12 a month, however it is paid every year at the same time as the enterprise plans are $25 a month, which offers you a free place and a gaggle of numerous new skills.

Now that we've have been given Included some of the internet's maximum well-known weblog net web websites, the subsequent query to answer is:

How can I begin a blog and make cash?

Based on the comparisons given above, WordPress.Org is with the aid of way of far the most superior and offers you charge on your cash. You can run advertisements free of charge, and you also have greater manage over your content fabric. You can strive to check out the other structures however take be conscious that inside the event you do alternate your thoughts and want emigrate your content material cloth material from specific structures to WordPress- you'd get into an entire load of inconvenience, a waste of time, attempt and not to mention cash. The greater posts you have got have been given and the higher the website site visitors, the more likely you'd need a weblog that offers you the introduced protection, the increasing capabilities similarly to the crucial manual.

So what do you do subsequent to kickstart your cash-making commercial organisation through your blog?

It boils all the manner right down to the ones following few steps:

1.   Choose a going for walks a blog region of interest

2.   Pick a platform

3.   Pick a website and hosting plan

4.   Monetize your blog

So which strolling a blog platform is pleasant for getting cash? It all boils proper down to your reason, dreams, and of route, fee variety. If you aren't fine, stick to a free plan first and explore the weblog's abilties after which pick out the only that exquisite suits your goals.

Choosing to move pinnacle fee have to best occur as soon as you've got a pretty appropriate concept of what you want in a weblog even if you have the fee range to transport top rate. This is due to the reality you would though need to make investments time, power further to assets to position inside the essential content material to peer if the weblog platform works for you or now not. No depend wide variety what the choice may be, select a platform that is straightforward to set up, dependable, strong, and has correct aid. All of this will benefit you in the end and save you cash as well as give you more headspace.

Other running a blog platforms or websites that you can try are SquareSpace, Contentful, Yola, Jekyll, Ghost in addition to LiveJournal.

What are the first rate going for walks a blog

systems for 2019, alternatively, and which may be great on your agency?

We positioned our coins's paintings on WordPress, Blogger in addition to Wix. WordPress.Org is in the end the way to move, and in the next few chapters, our awareness may be on installing region a WordPress blog, exploring your niche in addition to installing your running a weblog industrial business enterprise.

Chapter 12: WordPress - The Most Effective Platform to Make Money

WordPress is an smooth however powerful weblog and net internet web page content control system on the net these days. Ask any top bloggers what platform they use, and it will maximum in all likelihood be WordPress. This platform is an internet-based completely, open-deliver blog or net web page creation device coded in PHP. But all you want to apprehend approximately it is that it is easy to installation and start a blog or a internet internet web page.

Who uses WordPress?

A very valid question and to be honest, anyone can use it for any motive the least bit, together with a easy on line mag to a colourful excursion weblog or at the identical time as a records portal or political internet web site. Popular websites which includes CNN and Forbes use WordPress, and Fortune 500 groups which include UPS, Sony, and eBay use WordPress. WordPress is the maximum famous going for walks a weblog and internet internet site online CMS due to its many features, balance, and person-awesome navigating.

What's the distinction among WordPress.Com and WordPress.Org?

The one that separates the .Com web web page with the .Org internet web page is the internet web hosting provider. If you sign on for a .Org, then YOU host your personal net website or weblog using the offerings of an internet website hosting enterprise. WordPress.Org is the software program application that you can down load and set up into your net server. For the WordPress.Com website, the hosting is done via manner of WordPress, so there's no downloading or deciding to buy introduced web hosting or dealing with your very personal net server.

How do I start using WordPress?

WordPress requires no price the least bit, besides maybe a while. But essentially, there may be no need to purchase some thing in advance. It is in reality one hundred% unfastened. Opening a WordPress account is freed from path and having a internet website or blog is really unfastened. However, in case you would love to have your online net page a selected manner or particular coloration and to have some sure upgrades, then those updates require a few form of funding.

Benefits of Using WordPress

WordPress has many staggering capabilities; it clearly is why it the most desired net site and running a blog platform. Here are some blessings of using WordPress:

● Easy to join up

All you need to do is be part of up for a WordPress account the use of your electronic mail and password. There is a two-step verification manner that clients want to take a look at to verify. Also, most website hosting offerings help WordPress via a one-click on installation choice.

●Secure Open Source Network and Vibrant Community

WordPress is utilized by masses of people. Therefore, the network itself creates a huge database of loose subjects and plugins that you could take gain of to your website. Users can use the ones freebies, however there also are a number of top elegance themes and plugins that don't fee so much and are available prepared with exceptional manual from their companies.

What Kinds Of Websites Can WordPress Make?

When WordPress first materialized at the Internet, WordPress modified into created for the primary motive to create a blog in place of to create web sites. But way to changes in WordPress's center coding, this going for walks a weblog platform has come to be a huge environment filled with problems, plugins, and tool that permits really all and sundry to create any sort of blog or net website using WordPress.

Doing a quick Google are seeking now in 2019, you'd see that there are loads of web sites and blogs that use WordPress to strength up large exchange and commercial enterprise skills. Right now, WordPress is the maximum famous platform to create stunning and person-extraordinary eCommerce shops. With WordPress, you could construct:

- Business websites

- eCommerce stores

- Blogs

- Portfolios

- Resumes

- Forums

- Social networks

- Membership websites

Monetizing Your WordPress Site

There are plenty of strategies to monetize your WordPress net web site to make cash from it but a very good manner to do that, you need to decorate your net internet web page to make it smooth for human beings to do what you need them to do you on-internet web web page, whether or no longer or now not it is to look at your content material material fabric, to purchase your merchandise or to subscribe or sign on to your offerings.

Apart from those options above, most humans moreover start off with the use of AdSense commercials further to via companion packages. AdSense, that is operated with the resource of way of Google lets in you to vicinity your advertisements on your net web site and gets a fee each time humans click on on it. Through associate packages, in particular those via Amazon, it lets in you to link any product that Amazon consists of and also you get a fee while there's a purchase.

Making cash the use of a WordPress blog web website is possible, however you need to comprehend that it does take time, it's going to take try, and it's going to want a few form of funding. Once you get the dangle of it, at the same time as you get subjects set up, you'd be greater of a pro round your weblog.

Optimizing Your WordPress Site to Make Money

In this financial ruin, our interest on optimizing our weblog to make sure it is prepared to make cash or at least, making it much less difficult for your customers or your target market to do what you want them to do in your blog.

Making your net net website online Stand out

● Browsing experience

The facts you positioned into your web web site is what units it aside from a normal net website online on your very very own unique commerce one. Your essential motive is to make their surfing experience for your blog as seamless as feasible. The manner you may do that is to recognition your facts in the format and format, that's what most human beings will see after they go to your internet web page.

●Hover Link

Some small information you'd like to test out are topics which consist of the hover link. Most subjects characteristic a very specific coloration while the mouse is moved, or 'hovered' over a web page or publish or link. The component links and lessons also change coloration whilst the mouse hovers over it. This tells your users that this content material cloth is what they may be approximately to click on on on on.

What may your desire be? Would you need it to be the same colour? Do you want it to alternate? Do you need it underlined? These alternatives are a non-public preference if you would really like subjects to appearance a hint particular. These small details are layout elements that you can trade at any element for your internet site. WordPress' interface is as easy at the backend as it's far on the the front give up. You can also alternate the header and the footer phase, the hover sunglasses, and so on.

● Experiment with the manner your posts will appearance

While your net net website is new, you will now not have any internet web page visitors (or at the least targeted visitors) in your net website online online. So take this time to mess around with subjects. Create a blog submit to test to look how matters look. Check to appearance how this first put up will look on your property internet web page and first-rate-song any important data you'd like as which include font, font type as font length. Look on the layout and also see the way it fits to your internet site and if it's far readable.

● Utilizing Categories and tags

WordPress uses a data tool known as Categories or Tags that could help categorize your posts or related subjects collectively. As increasingly more posts are delivered, you may turn out to be creating extra tags or instructions and don't worry approximately this because of the truth tags and instructions are perfect. Each elegance will seem each in the footer or sidebar of your web page, relying on what layout you've selected. Archives additionally act the identical way. Your tags and instructions ought to be targeted on getting your products important and captured via seek engine advertising and marketing.

Optimizing Your Appearance Screen

●Choosing a Theme that suits your vicinity of interest

Ensuring that the difficulty you pick out out relates to your area of interest is crucial. This is due to the reality the problem count offers the overall appearance of your blog internet site on line, and this is in which you deliver existence in your internet site. Depending on what you want your internet site on-line to do, there are various problems that you could use to absolutely alternate the appearance of your net website online on-line. These problems are designed via way of WordPress builders and WordPress customers, and you may pick from masses of issues, a few unfastened, at the same time as a few are paid subjects. Each subject matter demonstrated below the Appearance segment is built to cater to a particular want for the person. For instance, some challenge topics are built to cater to a commercial enterprise form of internet website online whilst some subjects are made to characteristic snap shots and pix; some subjects are built to characteristic fashion and online retail while some are constructed to keep writing and poetry or prolonged articles.

To alternate the advent of your internet web page, all you need to do is click on on on on a topic can click on Purchase (if it is a paid problem depend) or Activate (if it's far a loose project matter).

Keep in mind that you may need to align the appearance of your net website online online with the identical branding that your enterprise makes use of. Your on-line individual wants to be the same with all the unique advertising and marketing and marketing angles that you rent to your communications and advertising strategies. The identical is going on your private weblog.

Planning your Website on your Business

Designing a internet internet site on line or a blog that makes a speciality of getting cash calls for making plans, and it dreams a strong and strategic plan. Although putting a internet web site or blog via WordPress is unfastened, you'd though want a few issue this is lasting, sustainable, and suits on the aspect of your business employer method. You may also additionally even want to determine if you would like net website hosting your very own net web page using WordPress.Org in any other case you'd rather use WordPress.Com.

Here are a few subjects to set up:

●What will you do along with your net website online on-line?

●What shape of content do you want on it?

●What enterprise technique are you planning to use on your net site?

●Who do you want to examine this?

●How frequently do you propose on posting and which include content material cloth?

Depending on what your net web site is supposed to do, you'll want to remember what sort of information you are willing to proportion and positioned up. You may also want to consist of a few contact facts so your traffic on your internet site can contact you- till you don't want them to.

●Choosing a Domain Extension

A place extension is the 3 letters after a dot that you see on a net web site link. This works for every the .ORG or .COM WordPress desire.

Usually, whilst you open a WordPress site, you'll frequently have your internet site online with a URL which includes this: www.Mynewsite.WordPress.Com. To alternate this with out the WordPress name in it, you may need to sign in your area, and this normally way figuring out to buy the net website hosting which WordPress offers.

But in advance than you could choose your location name, a word of advice- DO NOT attempt to change your net website to a fixed area except you're very positive of the route of your website online and the content material.

Make certain your WordPress website is inside the area of interest you need to cognizance and supply interest to. Making your WordPress net site on-line a sensible and profits-generating net website online requires vital studies for your aim keyword pool. Below said are a number of the assets you want to consider whilst registering your area:

•If you want a Business Website- if this website online is in your corporation, then a tremendous vicinity to check in your internet site may be a DOT COM as in .Com web website online, together with mynewsite.Com.

•If you need an accomplice advertising and marketing internet website, ensure your blog name relates for your region of interest

•If you need a Personal Website- Well it is your own private internet site so go along with some aspect you need, however the most famous is, of route, .Com.

•A non-Profit Website- for a non-profits internet web website, the excellent place call might be a .ORG.

•Information Website- a .Data, of course, can be the splendid!

There are hundreds of vicinity name extensions, but the maximum well-known ones are .Com, .Org, .Internet and .Data. And the ones are with out problems picked up with the aid of Google.

●Choosing the Right Domain Name

The domain call and the area extension pass hand in hand. Once you have determined in your domain extension, you want to discern out what you'd like to name your net page as a manner to be your area. Your place call is what your net web site's URL will include while a person types it inside the browser's cope with bar.

Here are a few essential elements to bear in thoughts at the same time as coming up in conjunction with your Domain Name:

●Matching Names: Essentially, the call of your site in addition to the URL should healthy.

●Short: So it's less difficult to hold in thoughts and may be typed into the browser

●Consistent Branding: Your domain is a reflected photo of your logo. Keep it steady and excellent.

•Memorable: Well, a internet internet website need to be easy to take into account and remarkable, so that you need it to paste the primary time while your visitors come on your website online.

•Catchy: It ought to be easy to pronounce and rolls off the tongue without difficulty. Your domain call need to moreover describe what you do.

Includes Keywords: Because you need it to be Search Engine Optimized.

Essentially you want it to be smooth to undergo in thoughts and easy to type. Your place name need to correspond with what your agency does or what your personal on-line time table is to your net internet page.

Customizing and Personalizing

To make your internet website online 100% your very very own, you may pick to personalize and personalize the problem remember. Usually, customization is accomplished on the fonts, sunglasses, and one-of-a-kind smooth layout elements with out changing the format of the website on line. To customise the difficulty you have were given decided on, you could skip lower back to the Appearance section and pick out the Customize hyperlink. Here, you have got the option of doing a selection of things for your internet internet site on line to make it sync in together with your branding dreams. Usually, most topics will can help you exchange the brand, sun shades, and backgrounds, the fonts, the header photo, the menus, and widgets.

If you are not professional in coding, fantastic to move away the customization to the chosen options. But in case you do apprehend to code and can take your net internet site on line's customization to some other level then pass ahead- there may be no stopping you and the sky's the limit!

•Widgets

You can discover the widgets section underneath appearance as nicely. Depending on the challenge you've got got selected, you could have a choice of widgets to pick from. Most widgets are the identical for maximum subjects, and a few are some extra precise ones based on the sort of topic you have got selected. Widgets are preset factors which can be delivered to a website to beautify its abilties and improve your internet internet site's potential.

Some of the equal widgets you will regularly discover in most of these topics are which embody Archives, Blog Stats, Calendar, Category Cloud, Facebook Page Plugin, Gallery, Gravatar, Image, Instagram, Milestone, Music Player and Twitter Timeline. Take study that widgets aren't Plugins, however they will be elements that beautify your website and add more functionality. Widgets assist with navigation and furthermore to decorate your connectivity on your social media. Widgets are pretty beneficial so that you have to add this for your net net web page.

To add a widget, truly go to the Widget phase, click on on the Add a Widget. From then on, you may see a listing of several widgets that you can upload for your internet web page. Click on the Widget you would like to feature after which click on on 'Save & Publish.'

●Menu

You can also exchange the Menu section of your internet website online. Menus are a vital element to any website. They offer a manner of navigating your net page and all your content material. You want your web page website online traffic to go through all your charming content, and the manner can they do it without knowledge in which to go and locate your content material material? That is when the menus come into play. If your menus and navigation are hard, your visitors will find out it difficult to discover your content material fabric, and this can result in excessive bounce charges- it simply is the form of website online visitors in your net web page, how lengthy they spend on it and how many posts they view earlier than leaving.

Menus commonly seem on the top of the internet site (because of the reality that's in which human beings appearance first). Sometimes, you can discover the menus on the net web page or perhaps at the lowest. This is notable as long as you know what you need your visitors to reputation on once they first come for your internet internet site.

Menus want to encompass pages like 'About' 'Contact,' 'Product,' 'Services' as a part of your primary menu. You can commonly get rid of or add pages to your menu steady with what your internet page calls for. Some menus and their placement on your internet site on line very masses depend upon your WordPress topic.

A specific menu has numerous developments which is probably:

• concise and minimalistic

- represents of all your website on-line's offerings

- very intuitive to use and smooth to navigate spherical your internet site

Keep the ones elements on your thoughts whilst arranging and operating in your menu, and you'll be ok.

- Plugins

As one-of-a-type in advance, Plugins are considered one of a kind from Widgets. Plugins are first-class available for WordPress.Org and are basically portions of code which may be written to carry out a very unique feature on your net page. For instance, the sharing plugin brought on your website allows you to percentage content material in the course of loads of social systems. The WordPress network has advanced a number of Plugins that help in search engine optimization, enhancing the safety of your internet web site online, keeping massive portfolios in addition to including touch office work or inquiry office work.

●Tags

Tags were much like commands besides the ones tags are precise to a placed up. Think of it like hashtagging an picture on Instagram or Twitter. These tags beneficial useful resource your web website online's site visitors in locating precise information and content material material for your internet site online extra without troubles.

●Your Profile

Oh, how can we ever forget about to talk about your profile page! Setting your WordPress profile is virtually easy, and one of the maximum natural things to complete even as developing your internet web page. You can normally edit and trade records to your Profile through taking place your 'Edit your Profile' segment positioned on the administrator show at the top proper nook of the display. Here, supply yourself a quick description and additionally upload to your social media hyperlinks.

In the profile image, all you need to do is upload an photo of your self or your Logo, and this can become your Gravatar account. Under this section, you could additionally manage your billing facts- if you need to buy any paid Widgets, Plugins, or issues, and you may moreover decide on the safety in your web website. WordPress gives its users the option of producing a sturdy password just so your net website online on-line is steady.

Bottom Line

Just start already! Sometimes the superb way of studying about WordPress is thru trial and errors. We all have many inhibitions whilst beginning some issue new, however most of these items are just starting up doors to failure.

Creating a website and generating sales or getting your content cloth accessible within the fastest way viable isn't any small feat. It takes an entire lot of tough artwork, advertising and marketing, and publicity to get people to recognize approximately your website and to get your services or products or certainly take a look at what you have got were given to mention. But with WordPress, this apparently difficult project is made easy. For the following couple of chapters, you'll discover more guidelines and hints to get your internet site up and rolling and bringing the sales.

Chapter 13: Setting up and Securing Your WordPress Blog

As with a few element that you got all the way down to do, you want to apprehend the fundamentals of running a blog or as a minimum the basics of WordPress. With WordPress, getting to know the basics is straightforward and smooth. While this financial ruin is not going to right into a step-with the aid of using using-step guide on the way to set up a WordPress blog, it's going to, but, popularity on the crucial factors of installing a WordPress weblog, in particular wherein safety is concerned.

To get you began, there are a few things to check the Dashboard. Think of the Dashboard much like the command middle of your net website on line. This is in which you may trade the arrival and experience of your internet website online on-line, determine who can submit matters, who can commentary, you may regulate the manner the internet website appears- the entirety! Firstly, WordPress is constructed with an clean consumer-interface which means that that blog and internet net website owners can replace net web page content material and characteristic their blog quick and resultseasily. However, earlier than you begin posting or improving or customizing your internet page, proper proper right here are some fundamentals to undergo:

Logging In

Begin thru logging into your dashboard, that is the lower returned forestall of your internet website. Think of the backend because the behind the curtain location of a diploma production. The backend wants to be running well in advance than some thing earlier can perform efficiently. Your login can be accessed via the WP-ADMIN. You can also type in www.WordPress.Com and embody for your log in facts which are your username and password.

View Site Link

Upon logging in, you may be at the Administration display show, which is also called the Dashboard. This is the control panel of your internet site on line wherein you could change, edit, delete, upload, and regulate subjects. This is in that you put together your complete net website online on line.

At the top of the show show, you may locate the toolbar. To view your internet page, all you need to do is click on on on the link that indicates you Site call. This will take you right now in your WordPress internet site- a few issue call that you have you ever ever given it. Look at it and spot what you want approximately the layout and the colors, the navigation panel. Don't fear approximately changing it now, although- you could constantly try this every time.

Trying out your WordPress Site

Now if you are new to WordPress, take it slow to check your website on-line in advance than converting a few element and trying to decide out how the whole thing works. It is normally suitable to check out the number one net website online on line, so you understand what the distinction is amongst posts and pages, menus, and widgets. The layout in your internet website on line is how your internet web page will appearance in look. Usually, the layout will correspond with the difficulty you select out to your website on-line. As noted earlier. Most layouts will incorporate the ones fundamentals:

Header

•Footer

•Menu

•Title & Tagline

- Links

- Titles

Posts

Most posts should have a call, and the understand will consist of a date of whilst the placed up has been published. In the layout of the put up, there may be a body where most of the content material will bypass on. There also can be a few tagging which you need to encompass, that's known as placed up metadata. This commonly consists of statistics approximately the located up that may be brief picked up with the resource of Google, so every time someone searches for some factor on the internet and your placed up has a tag associated with the keyword, it is going to reveal up in are in search of outcomes.

Pages

Pages range from posts. Pages are greater static, and this usually is things like About Us, Contact Us or Sign Up for Mailing List. These pages, at the same time as static continues to be editable down the street. But make certain the statistics you positioned on those pages are matters which you need all traffic for your internet net web site to have a take a look at really so they need to be constant and correct. Page titles describe the statistics you want to proportion for your net page.

Sidebar

At the sidebar for your net web website, you will typically see all of the sections of your net web page. You will discover such things as Recent Posts and Recent Comments, Archives of route in addition to the Categories section. You may additionally find out RSS feeds and the logout hyperlink. People will use this to move round your website on-line to find out various things for your net website online. You will want this, and this is vital now not only for finding records for your internet site however also, so your internet site on line seems to be one of the top five on Google's listings.

User Profile

When you click on on on it, the show will supply you to a list of customers which might be the usage of the account. There may want to multiple users assigned to the internet site, but there can pleasant be one or two directors. Multiple customers for a net site mean that a couple of character has get right of entry to to to the net website on-line. However, because the administrator of the internet internet web page, you may be capable of manage what splendid clients can or cannot do. You can assign roles which include Contributor, Author, Editor, Administrator, or Follower. Each of these titles has specific roles. The Author can high-quality receive and edit content material fabric but can't exchange the arrival of the net website. The Administrator can do all of the above and characteristic general manipulate of the net page. As the net website online proprietor, you get to determine who may also have get right of access to to what segments for your net website online online.

Hosting and Securing Your WordPress Website

For a net internet website to attain achievement and cater to the massive influx of net website online site traffic, it desires right web hosting and protection. Now which you have familiarized yourself with the backend section of WordPress and the various methods in posting, handling and customizing your net web site, it's far now time to check an regularly ignored but pretty important detail of a internet site- internet hosting and protection.

Web Hosting

A precise internet net website hosting machine will and may enhance your search engine advertising as well as energy up sales and placement visits. WordPress offers numerous sorts of web hosting options which includes Free, Shared, VPS, Dedicated, and controlled WordPress internet hosting. So what web hosting would possibly match your internet site goals? Here are some terrific tried and tested net net web hosting agencies that you may use to your site:

●BLUEHOST

This corporation is one of the oldest net net web hosting corporations at the internet, starting way lower lower again in 1996. BlueHost is a logo that comes up every time there may be a want to host a WordPress internet website. They may be taken into consideration the dependable WordPress recommended hosting company. BlueHost gives free place similarly to a loose web website builder that includes cutting-edge templates that you could pick out from. Many WP novice users prefer to use BlueHost as it also comes with a unique provide.

●HOSTGATOR

HostGator is likewise a completely well-known net hosting commercial enterprise enterprise, and it hosts over eight million domains. HostGator offers and smooth to set up one-click on on WordPress set up, and it additionally comes with 24 hours assist.

●DREAMHOST

Been throughout the corporation for 18 years, DreamHost could be very widely known for its web hosting simplicity. You get a custom dashboard and a one-click on WordPress installation in addition to commonplace computerized WordPress updates to hold your net web page in pinnacle state of affairs. It also has unlimited location and limitless bandwidth and free SSDs, which makes your internet page 2 hundred% faster to get right of entry to and navigate. There are not any installation fees, and in addition they provide place registration with out cost.

●INMOTION

InMotion has been stated to provide great and dependable performance, especially for industrial business enterprise net websites. It has an award-prevailing technical assist team with ninety nine% uptime. InMotion's web hosting talents and programs cater high-quality for terribly lively bloggers and gives giant scalability for the blogger's growth.

Securing your WordPress Website

Malicious attacks to your website on-line are commonplace, and masses, specifically while you gather and keep sensitive statistics that is why securing your website is essential.

There are many strategies of managing malicious assaults, and maximum professionals will allow you to understand that there may be no ONE sure manner of doing it and in fact, the first rate manner to constant your internet internet page is by way of manner of the usage of the use of numerous techniques and strategies. Just like how you lock your gate, stable your own home with CCTVs, and actually have get right of access to codes and alarm structures for your private home, the same issue works to your net website.

Sometimes you can enjoy malicious assaults, however maximum of these assaults can be subjects which you in no way found out have been taking place. So on this phase, we are able to speak about improving the safety of your internet website on line. Take take a look at which you do now not need to do all of it as it very thousands is predicated upon on what you located in your net site on line.

A) HIDING YOUR SITE'S LOGIN PAGE

If your internet web site allows character logins, then malicious login attempts are unfortunately unavoidable. Your login web page wishes to be effortlessly found on your net website just so your customers can get proper of entry to it outcomes. However, you can do unique subjects to defend in competition to malicious attempts which we're in a position to talk in some time. But for now not, we can recognition on hiding your login net page due to the reality this is one manner of slicing down at the malicious login attempts. A virus that can't find out your login internet web page will no longer be capable of log into it.

If you aren't eager on hiding your login web page, then you may furthermore area in certainly one of a type security measures which include the usage of a Captcha code verification. This calls for putting in and configuring an exceptional safety plugin. Obscuring your login internet web page is a legitimate protection degree, mainly when it's far used as part of a aggregate of protection technique. Here's how to disguise your internet website online on line login page:

Strategy 1- Installing WordPress its personal Directory

Back up your net web page on-line and store it someplace in which you cannot via the use of twist of destiny modify or delete it. Next, set up the WPS Hide Login plugin. This plugin allows you to safely and without problem trade the URL of your login net page to almost some thing which you want. This plugin does now not rename or exchange any documents in your device; neither does it rewrite any codes. All this plugin does is intercepts internet web page requests, and this will be used on all WordPress internet web sites. By using this plugin, the WP-Admin listing and the wp-login.Php page becomes inaccessible to anyone besides you. Create a URL this is specific however with out hassle remember best through you. If you deactivate this plugin, this can deliver lower back the login internet internet page to the equal true u . S . A . That it became earlier than.

Strategy 2- Using WP Hide & Security Enhancer

WP Hide & Security Enhancer is likewise plugins that assist find the reality that your internet internet web page is on foot on WordPress. The reason why you need to cowl the reality that your internet site is on WordPress is so you can create custom login URLs while truely disabling the default URLs. Apart from that, this plug additionally boasts over one thousand active installs, and on the same time as this isn't an notable big variety, it's far certainly a massive sufficient sample size that may be used for client critiques. Ratings were robust and regular, because of this making WP Hide and Security Enhancer an exceptional plugin to have.

Strategy three- Cerber Limit Login Attempts

Another well-known plugin for better safety may be the Cerber plugin which essentially limits login tries. Currently, it's far actively used on over 10,000 net web sites and has a rating of four.Nine out of five stars with the aid of the use of its clients. Apart from proscribing login tries, this plugin also can conceal the standard URL so that you can use a custom designed one as an alternative. By a long way, this is the maximum stable and easiest preference favored with the resource of the WordPress network with greater than seven-hundred,000 energetic installs.

B) WEBSITE LOCKDOWN AND BANNING USERS

Another manner of securing your internet web page is through which encompass a lockdown feature, in particular on the identical time as there had been failed login tries. Most online banking structures do this. Lockdown capabilities remedy a exceptional hassle it's to restriction or altogether prevent non-forestall brute stress attempts. If there may be a hacking try thru manner of the use of the wrong passwords repetitively (at the least three instances), the internet web page right now gets locked down, and you will acquire a notification of unauthorized hobby.

One such plugin that lets in this option is the iThemes Security plugin which has been spherical for pretty a while and is desired via the WordPress network. Not quality does this plugin offer the lockdown characteristic, but it moreover allows you to specify the kind of failed attempts, and then the plugin moreover bans the attacker's IP address right away, so you do now not need to worry about this hacker once more.

C) TWO FACTOR AUTHENTICATION

Nowadays in case you test, even electronic mail offerings provide -step authentication techniques collectively with the one hired via the use of Gmail or maybe Facebook. Called the 2FA, this is a few other excellent safety characteristic. The man or woman wanting to log into a website gives the crucial login records for 2 one-of-a-type factors. The net internet site owner includes a preference what those sincerely one in every of a kind additives may be. Usually, it's going to probably be logging inside the password after which answering a mystery query or a code or a set of characters.

D) USING YOUR EMAIL AS LOGIN

Using your electronic mail may look like a much less solid manner, however in truth, it is actually greater regular. Usernames are plenty less tough to anticipate, whilst e-mail IDs aren't. Also, beginning a WordPress account calls for a completely unique e mail

ID; as a end result, logging in via this identifier is lots more constant.

E) ADJUSTING YOUR PASSWORD

Changing your password as quickly as every three months is usually recommended for all forms of login device, specially your banking on-line bills and web web sites which you commonplace all of the time. If converting it honestly isn't exquisite for you, then mess around with the password by means of manner of the usage of changing it to lowercase or uppercase, including numbers or unique characters in case your net page permits it. No idea what to apply as a password? Then attempt a password generator!

F) SECURING YOUR ADMIN DASHBOARD

The maximum attractive a part of a net website online for the hacker is the admin dashboard due to the fact right right right here, the hacker receives to control your internet website! Dashboards are generally the maximum blanketed section of the whole internet site, and it's going to in all likelihood be the hardest to get via for the hacker. To decorate the security of this segment, proper right here's what you may do:

- Protecting the WP-Admin list

If this factor is hacked, then your complete system can be compromised and damaged. One manner of stopping this from taking place is through manner of password protective your wp-admin list. This method that the net internet site proprietor or number one administrator for the net site on-line can only get right of get right of entry to to the dashboard through a -step authentication approach. One password protects the login page at the equal time as the alternative protects the admin phase. The proprietor of the internet site on-line can also unblock certain additives so different customers may also moreover have get proper of entry to to it thru a one password device, but the owner can lock the rest of the internet page which stores more touchy statistics.

● Using SSL to encrypt information

SSL refers to Secure Socket Layer, and you can put into impact the SSL certificate to make certain a greater solid management panel for your net site. SSL lets in everyday records transfer between browsers in addition to servers, for that reason making it a venture for hackers to infiltrate a connection or spoof sensitive statistics. Getting an SSL on your internet site is not a hard problem to do. All you want to do is purchase one at a committed company, or you may furthermore test this along with your internet web hosting corporation who can hook you up with a carrier issuer. Most regularly, SSL certificates are blanketed as an non-compulsory object in maximum internet hosting packages.   G) CHANGING THE ADMIN USERNAME

One of the most inclined topics you could do to weaken your protection is with the useful resource of the use of 'admin' due to the reality the username for the principle administrator position on your net net web site. This is because it's far a quite sincere and easy to guess username that hackers will no question use. All they want to recognise now could be your password and then get their hands on your records. Again, you can use the iThemes Security plugin to prevent malicious login attempts because of the truth this may right away cast off any IP deal with that attempts to use admin due to the fact the username.

H) MONITORING YOUR FILES

Monitoring your internet site hobby is critical. You may additionally moreover furthermore need to install a plugin which embody Acunetix WP Security or Wordfence at the way to assist you to display the modifications in your net websites' documents. Also, all of your internet web page's records and statistics is saved within the database, and right here are a few approaches that you may cope with it:

- Changing the WordPress database desk prefix- WordPress has a wp- prefix that is used actually with the aid of the usage of the WordPress database so that it will decorate the security, exchange it to a few factor unique which includes mywp- or wpnew- or wpnewsite-. Plugins can also do that for you, which consist of the WP-DBManager that allows you exchange your plugins into some element specific with only some clicks.

I) BACKUP YOUR SITE REGULARLY

No do not forget what security enhancements you have got got and the way stable your internet website is, it's going to in no way damage to make room for enhancements. So attempt backing up your net page at least as quickly as per week or each day in case you need to at an off-website on line backup this is the extraordinary answer. Having a backup will will let you restore your WordPress web page to a operating united states of america at any time, specifically if there's been a hack or harm. VaultPress thru Automattic is a outstanding plugin that can assist do this for you. This plugin backs up your internet site at 30-minute intervals so you can repair quite effortlessly must a few difficulty awful show up. Restoration absolutely takes one click on on, and it additionally tests your net website for any malware and sends an alert if it detects a few difficulty fishy.

J) SETTING UP STRONG PASSWORDS

Your fundamental databases require an exceedingly robust password and as commonly, use a mixture of characters, numbers pinnacle and reduce case alphabets. Try to anticipate out of the field and use gadgets or locations or topics which have absolutely no reference to your website. For instance, you can use a password combination of your desired meals, music, fragrance, band name, or possibly an area you visited before. Special characters which includes the asterisk mark or the exclamation mark make for sturdy passwords.

K) PROTECTING YOUR wp-config.Personal home web page FILE

This file extension holds all of the essential statistics approximately your WordPress net website online, and as a matter of reality, this is the most critical detail to your website's root listing. Compromise this, and also you lose loads of things for your website. By shielding the personal home page record, you are shielding the very middle of your WordPress weblog. When you shield this middle issue of your website, you're then making it highly difficult for hackers to break the protection of your web website because of the reality the wp-config.Hypertext Preprocessor document is impossible to get proper of entry to via them.

Do you observed that is tough to solid?

Think once more. Securing or defensive your report is definitely very clean. All you need to do is exchange the region of your wp-config.Personal domestic web page document by way of way of the usage of taking it and shifting it on a better stage than your root listing. Will the server be capable of get right of entry to this if it's miles saved some region else? Well with the all-new and advanced WordPress shape, the configuration file settings had been programmed at the satisfactory priority list so no matter the fact that this personal home page record is saved one degree above the idea list, WordPress and pleasant WordPress can find it.

L) BAR ANY FILE EDITING

If your net web page is a multi-person net page, and if a few different character has administrative get right of get entry to to for your WordPress dashboard, then they will edit, exchange, put off and alter any documents which can be part of your WordPress set up which moreover manner deleting or adding plugins or changing concern matters. So to prevent this from going on, you want to disallow record editing. By doing this, if a hacker has one way or the alternative obtained admin access on your

WordPress dashboard, they will despite the fact that not be able to regulate any shape of record.

M) CONNECT YOUR SERVERS PROPERLY

You should superb connect with your server through SFTP or SSH at the equal time as putting in place your net web page. SFTP is the most favored way over the traditional FTP as it has higher protection competencies and none of these can be placed within the great FTP record. Connecting your server using the SFTP way ensures solid facts and files transfer. This is also an non-compulsory characteristic in most internet website hosting packages.